A MORE *BEAUTIFUL* WAY TO LIVE

"In this gem of a book, Bethaney Wilkinson invites us to tend to our lives—to offer more care to our spirits, more curiosity to our longings, and more space to our bodies. Grab a notebook as you read. Bethaney's questions helped me diagnose my own burnout, and her guidance on rituals provides a road map to exit crisis mode."

—**Beth Silvers**, cohost of Pantsuit Politics; coauthor of *I Think You're Wrong (But I'm Listening)* and *Now What?*

"For those seeking a sustainable cadence for living, *A More Beautiful Way to Live* offers practices for soul-strength and resilience, grounded in the wisdom of the natural world. Writing with the gentleness of an experienced spiritual director, Bethaney Wilkinson is a kind and thoughtful companion, inviting us to tend our inner lives with care, trusting that patient, diligent work to ripple outward into communal good."

—**Krissy Kludt**, author of *I Could Walk Forever and Know So Little*; executive director of Writing the Wild

"I couldn't put this book down. I saw my own journey and those of my friends reflected in its pages. Bethaney invites us to slow down, tune out the noise, and reconnect with what truly matters in a world that pushes us to keep striving and performing. She writes with remarkable clarity, blending her personal story with practical guidance and actionable tools for anyone seeking a more intentional life—*a more beautiful way*. The book is both raw and uplifting, capturing the realities of burnout, the ache for rest, and the courage it takes to choose a more meaningful path. Whether you are overwhelmed, searching for direction, or simply ready for change, this book will leave you empowered and inspired."

—**Faitth Brooks**, podcaster and author of *Remember Me Now*

A MORE *BEAUTIFUL* WAY TO LIVE

Nine Practices to Unlearn Habits of Anxiety, Fear, and Urgency

BETHANEY B. WILKINSON

a division of Baker Publishing Group
Grand Rapids, Michigan

Published by Brazos Press
a division of Baker Publishing Group
Grand Rapids, Michigan
BrazosPress.com

Printed in the United States of America

Library of Congress Cataloging-in-Publication Data
Names: Wilkinson, Bethaney B., 1990– author
Title: A more beautiful way to live : nine practices to unlearn habits of anxiety, fear, and urgency / Bethaney B. Wilkinson.
Description: Grand Rapids, Michigan : Brazos Press, a division of Baker Publishing Group, [2026] | Includes bibliographical references.
Identifiers: LCCN 2025029613 | ISBN 9781587436581 paperback | ISBN 9781493452217 ebook
Subjects: LCSH: Spiritual life | Contemplation | Time—Religious aspects | Mind and body—Religious aspects
Classification: LCC BL624 .W565 2026
LC record available at https://lccn.loc.gov/2025029613

Some names and details have been changed to protect the privacy of the individuals involved.

Cover design by Lindy Kasler

The author is represented by The Christopher Ferebee Agency, www.christopherferebee.com.

Baker Publishing Group publications use paper produced from sustainable forestry practices and postconsumer waste whenever possible.

26 27 28 29 30 31 32 7 6 5 4 3 2 1

To Alex, my love, thank you for
teaching me the art of going slowly

CONTENTS

FOREWORD

KAITLIN B. CURTICE

When I began reading this book, I noticed two things: I took multiple deep breaths, and I began to sway left to right, something I do when I am trying to calm and comfort myself. That is the energy that Bethaney creates in the world, both in person and in her writing. She is an agent of care, a teacher of rest and paying attention.

What I want you to know as you begin this journey is that you can trust Bethaney. She is a guide, a teacher, a fierce woman who cares and loves deeply. She practices care for herself, you, and the world around us, and you'll feel that as you step into these pages and words. You can lean in with all of yourself, showing up as you are and asking the deepest questions you can ask, and you will be met with kindness. Don't be afraid.

As you read, I want you to notice some of the themes that are so apparent in this book, like presence, slowing down, acknowledgment of where you are, gentleness with all the versions of yourself, and the power of dreaming about the future you hope for.

Writer and psychotherapist Clarissa Pinkola Estés once wrote, "I urge you, ask you, gentle you, to please not spend your spirit dry by bewailing these difficult times. Especially do not lose hope. Most particularly because, the fact is—we were made for these times."[1]

I come back to these words constantly to remind myself that difficult moments in history have appeared to us before, and they will again. Our journey as humans is to do exactly what this book suggests—to live a more beautiful way, a more tender way, a more compelling and connected way.

The power of a book like this is that it is both timeless and timely. We need a reminder right now of how to survive in a world of crumbling empires and rising fear, anger, outrage, and, yes, beauty and love. And we need this book when things are calmer, when we are blissfully happy and hope to stay grounded even in bliss. That, to me, is what makes a book so meaningful, and Bethaney provides that.

A beautiful life is about adventure, but not just in the sense of sports or going to destinations that instill both fear and awe in us. I mean adventure as in showing up to every space we inhabit with a deep sense of purpose and care. That's the beautiful way we long for. I want to leave you with some words you're going to encounter in these pages as you trek deeper into the journey, because these words sum everything up so beautifully.

Read these words like a meditation. Let images and feelings seep into your bones, and don't turn away from what they bring up in you—in fact, hold all of it with tenderness, like a seed, because that is the sacred place from which your life will grow.

> A more beautiful way to live is a trek into the heart of your life. Much of the journey is boggy and messy. Making the descent into this place within requires inspiration and guidance. It takes courage to face limiting beliefs, to ask for help, and to tend to your pain. It takes self-awareness and a strong knowledge of

your body to move at a pace that keeps you advancing even when the trail becomes slippery or feels insecure. And perhaps more than anything, you must be able to hear your soul's longing, like the waterfall's roar, drawing you further down and deeper in, all in hopes of reaching that magical, sun-kissed place of sustenance and true rest.

Onward, together.

INTRODUCING

A MORE BEAUTIFUL WAY TO LIVE

Much of modern life draws us into a pace that feels frenetic and into patterns of urgency that create chaos in our souls. It's as if we are holding hands with anxiety and fear in nearly every part of our lives. It's the experience of being scattered and untethered—like no matter how many hours we have in a day, it never seems to be the amount we need. Maybe you've felt it before, the sleeplessness and the worry. The perpetual sense that you're never doing enough. The fear that if you stop moving for even one second, all the good and beautiful things you're dreaming of may fall apart. Sometimes the chaos manifests as aches in our bodies or as emotional reactivity in our relationships. Sometimes this inner chaos shows up as an inability to rest, to pause, or to take a full deep breath. Sometimes we know we're scattered because we can't seem to focus on a task or even relax our minds when a day's work is done. I've been there. Maybe you've been there too. Maybe this is where you are right now—scattered, untethered, anxious, and afraid.

I want you to know there is another way to live.

I started dreaming about "a more beautiful way," not really even knowing what this way was or would become, in my late twenties. It was then I realized that both the pace of my life and the intensity of my desire to change the world had me on a trajectory toward burnout and despair. The urgency culture of my world—I was living in the city of Atlanta, working full-time, going to grad school part-time, volunteering in my downtime, all while trying to keep up with friends and family—paired with my own disordered attachments to achievement left me feeling miserable and exhausted. I started to wonder if there was another way for me to exist on the earth. I also started to wonder if and how our fast-paced culture was shaping even our best efforts toward collective healing and change. I'd been leading a project focused on racial justice and organizational development, and while the project attracted a growing audience, I was crumbling on the inside. I was burning out in my effort to create good work in the world, and I couldn't stand up under the weight of the project's growth. It seemed to me that if I and others were burning out and diminishing in our ability to love and honor the humanity of our neighbors, friends, and enemies, then surely something was awry. Surely there had to be a way to do good work without losing our soul-deep connections to ourselves, to one another, and to the Creator who sustains our very lives.

In addition to this mismatch between the public expression of my work and my inner chaos, I was also wading through the complexities of having been diagnosed with uterine fibroids. I'd never experienced anything quite like them before, and for the first time in my adult life, I was forced to confront how significantly the functioning of my reproductive system impacted my life. My heart, mind, soul, and body were crying out for healing. I was hungry for a different way to experience my life and the people around me. I wanted to heal so that I could show up to the tasks of loving others well from a place of nourishment, support, and rest instead of from a place of worry and depletion. I was tired of being tired and wondered if "a more beautiful way" was possible.

What Is a More Beautiful Way to Live?

A more beautiful way is a framework for living that is characterized by three elements: being grounded, being present, and receiving and accepting the life you've been given. This way invites you to change not only how you live but also how you think, how you experience time, and how you orient your inner disposition to the world around you.

Being grounded, the first characteristic element of the beautiful way, is the opposite of feeling scattered and untethered. Groundedness is marked by feeling at peace in your life and in your body. When I think of being grounded, my mind goes to the large oak tree standing in my front yard. The oak tree is firmly planted, settled, and at home in the earth. It bends in the wind, loses branches in storms, and drops leaves each fall—but it is largely immovable in the ways that matter most. Being grounded is waking up in the morning peacefully resolved in your heart and mind about what's most important to do that day and mindfully putting your hands to the tasks in front of you. It's taking a deep breath before a difficult conversation, standing assured in your perspective while graciously honoring the humanity of the person sitting across from you. You know you're living a more beautiful way when you feel firmly planted, settled, and at home in the earth—even as the storms come and the seasons change.

The second element of this framework for living is being present, which is a mental, emotional, relational, and spiritual experience in which all your energies are held in the here and now. Instead of ruminating on the past or obsessively trying to control the future, you fix your mind and heart on what's right in front of you. This is a radical act, as technology masterfully draws us out of our present lives and into online worlds being curated for us. If you don't want to be present in your everyday life, you have a world of distractions at your fingertips. Living a more beautiful way, however, acknowledges how distraction perpetuates anxiety and fear in our lives and chooses presence instead, even when it's painful. If this sounds challenging, that's because it can be. Much of modern living doesn't make it easy for us to be present, especially for the tough parts of the human condition. My goal is to walk you through practices that will help you be present in your real life, even on the difficult days.

The third defining element of a more beautiful way of living is receiving and accepting your life as it is, as it's been given. This requires a tremendous amount of trust. If you're anything like me, you may bristle at this idea, especially if you're an overachiever who thrives on setting personal goals and accomplishing them. Believe me when I say this element is an ongoing challenge for me. I tend to fight and push and do everything in my power to make my life what I think it should be. But a more beautiful way of living welcomes life as it unfolds in surprising, challenging, and unexpected ways. It's about trusting that even the most challenging seasons carry much-needed wisdom in them. Receiving is being open to what your life wants to teach you, and accepting is a practice of surrender and trust. Receiving and accepting your life doesn't mean you never make changes or adjustments. It means that rather than trying to force and control your life, which often makes for more anxiety, you find peace in the chaos and, as cheesy as it sounds, go with the flow. The insights in this book will teach you how.

The Journey Before You

If you feel scattered, anxious, and fearful, my aim is to guide you into a life that is grounded, present, and open to your ever-emerging story. If your daily life feels as if you're running in forested wilderness with no sense of how to find your way out, the practices you will learn in these pages will lead you into a clearing where you can take a deep breath for the first time in a long time.

This book features nine practices for living a more beautiful way and is broken into three sections: groundwork, cultivation, and sustenance. Groundwork contains the foundational practices that will teach you how to face the reality of your life as it is. Cultivation focuses on welcoming new habits of self-management into your life. Sustenance is about maintaining an embodied way of being for the long haul. Within each of these three sections, we will loosely focus on three themes: time, body, and soul. Imagine these three themes as concentric circles. Time is the outermost circle and is defined as "a measurable period during which an action, process, or condition exists or continues."[1] We start with time because much of what makes for a scattered and anxious existence has to do with our pace of living. Both reclaiming our time and thinking about time in new ways create the conditions for groundedness, presence, and a trusting openness to emerge. Body is the second circle, as our bodies exist within time. Our bodies are limited in their capacity but profound in the wisdom they carry. As we seek to learn what it takes to live a more beautiful way, we will return again and again to the wisdom and needs of our bodies as a guide. The third and innermost circle is the soul, which I define as the inner life. Within your body and experienced in time, your inner life, or soul, is a place deep within. It's where you converse with yourself, where you reflect on your life, where you experience your emotions, and from where you speak your most honest truths and needs. We live both from the outside in (i.e., *time* influences our *bodies*, which influence our *souls*) and from the inside out (i.e., our *souls* influence our *bodies*, which influence how we experience *time*). If the scattered, anxious, and fearful life is the life we are leaving behind, and the grounded, present, and openhearted life is what we're after, then practices concerning time, body, and soul are the means that will get us there.

I've chosen to frame this way of living as a more "beautiful" way, as opposed to any number of other descriptors I could have chosen, because it is when I encounter the truly beautiful that my inner pace slows down and my senses stand at attention. Beauty, in my view, doesn't have a singular expression, but the soul knows when it has encountered something timeless, magnificent, and eternal. Many years ago, I had the pleasure of traveling to Boulder, Colorado. One night during our stay, my husband, Alex, and I drove outside the city to take in the stars. We pulled off on the side of the road, not a light in sight, and stood with our gaze set on the heavens. I'd never seen anything like it. Stars upon stars upon stars. I felt small, inspired, delighted, and overwhelmed all at once. I encountered the truly beautiful in that moment, and my soul knew it full well. I felt settled on the inside. I could breathe deeply and easily. It was as though all the worries in my heart faded for a moment and I was completely aware of my innate worth as a created being in the universe.

Such moments have the potential to rewrite our inner narratives about what it means to lead a grounded, present life. The beautiful washes over us gently and constantly, and in due time it softens our edges and changes our form. We encounter the beautiful in a loved one's smile. We encounter the beautiful when watching waves crash upon the shore. We encounter the beautiful when we enter the nave of a finely adorned sanctuary. When I contemplate the beautiful, I'm reminded of time beyond time—that mysterious, liminal space where we encounter the divine. The beautiful invites us to view our days in light of a grander reality. In contemplating the beautiful, I find permission to slow down, to be small, to say no, to pause, and to let go—all expressions of a more beautiful way. We get to unlearn habits of anxiety, fear, and urgency and put on practices of slowing down, of noticing, and of cultivating lives of connection to what matters most.

At the end of each part of this book, you'll find a "Pause & Reflect" section that includes a series of questions for you to take to your journal or into a conversation with friends. My goal with these questions is to help you slow down, experience calm in your body, and cultivate an experience of wholeness and peace in your soul.

With Gratitude to My Teachers

A more beautiful way to live is both a path I stumbled upon and a path on which I've had many guides. I want to honor their voices here because much of the wisdom you'll encounter in the following pages flows from the wisdom of many teachers who preceded me. As I moved from leading a fretful life into living a more tethered and centered one, I was fortunate to find myself in the world of Christian contemplation, an old and much cherished spiritual orientation in which people throughout the ages embraced silence, slowness, and stillness in order to awaken to the presence of the holy in their everyday lives. By reading authors like Parker Palmer, Barbara Holmes, and Cole Arthur Riley, I began building a worldview that held space for both a longing for depth and a desire to leave a positive impact on the world around me. In fact, through their work, I learned that contemplation and engagement with the world can be held together in beautiful and enriching ways. In addition to entering the ancient stream of Christian contemplation, I also began welcoming into my orbit voices like those of Robin Wall Kimmerer, Wendell Berry, Drew Lanham, and Leah Penniman—all folks who've dedicated their lives to knowing, loving, and tending the natural world. These lineages nourished me as I worked my way through despair toward healing.

In guiding you on how to actualize this way for yourself, I want to be honest that there is no magic formula or framework for living that can shield us from encountering the pain, loss, and disappointments that find their way to our doorsteps. Life can be unbelievably difficult. However, the hope of living a more beautiful way is that it will help us endure and will sustain us in the realities of life. We are striving to be like the oak tree—strong, firmly rooted, fruitful, and, though vulnerable to the winds and storms of life, able to withstand them.

Set an Intention

As we begin, I invite you to pause, close your eyes, and take a deep breath. I invite you to consider why you picked up this book and what you're hoping to take away from your time in these pages. As your purpose and aim become clear, I invite you to make a note, mentally or in the margin, about what you're hoping for as we begin this adventure. Setting an intention is a powerful way to guide your process through this book toward what is most meaningful to you.

Take another breath.

With hope and possibility, let us discover a more beautiful way to live.

PART ONE

GROUNDWORK

One

EMBRACING SLOW TIME

How did I end up here?

The lights were blinding, as their fluorescent beams bounced off the white, sterile emergency room walls. The cold metal edges of the hospital bed kept me confined and still as the nurse buzzed around me. He was preparing me for the procedure. I was doing my best to remain calm, confined, and still on the inside.

The truth: I was afraid.

How did I end up here? I thought to myself again.

The question reverberated in my mind like words spoken loudly into a cave, echoing back to me my own sense of disappointment and confusion. Emergencies of any kind have this effect on the human spirit. We are naturally disoriented by the travesties or inconveniences we don't see coming, and yet life is full of them.

This day had started out like most other days. I had a standard checkup at the doctor. I'd always experienced myself as relatively well, fit, able to come and go and do as I please. I arrived at the clinician's office and flowed through the motions of a regular appointment. My blood was drawn for basic testing, my vital signs were captured for my chart, I chatted with the physician about how I was doing, and then I went on my way. Easy.

I made my way out to the car and headed home. Within moments, my cell phone was ringing. I answered, "Hi, this is Bethaney."

"Ms. Wilkinson," the doctor said, "you need to head to the emergency room right away. We received your initial blood test results, and your hemoglobin levels are critically low. We're surprised you were able to walk into our office this morning. Head to the emergency room and tell them you need a blood transfusion immediately."

The doctor's voice trailed off, and I was sent into a spiraling haze. It was just like those moments in movies when someone gets news that takes their breath away and the lens blurs for a time.

How did I end up here, sitting on a hospital bed, waiting for an emergency procedure I didn't see coming?

My body was speaking. It was calling me to slow down, as it had been doing for quite some time, but finally I had ears to hear.

A few months prior to the moment I found myself in a cold hospital bed, I had moved through another confluence of crises. I, along with the rest of the world, received word of a coming pandemic. My office shut down quickly and unexpectedly. Leaders of communities small and large began rolling out rules, boundaries, conditions, and confinements meant to slow death's creep across our country. Overnight, nearly every aspect of my life, and really all our lives, changed drastically. Children and teachers were no longer in schools. Restaurants closed, and the ability to connect and laugh across shared meals with friends, family, neighbors, and lovers ceased for a time.

Families were required to reorganize, retool, and reimagine daily routines. Some households strengthened under the pressure; others fell apart. Jobs were lost and abilities to make ends meet were threatened, if not dissolved altogether. Meanwhile, I, along with the rest of the world, was struggling to make sense of it all.

What does this mean? What do we do? How do we move forward? How did we end up here?

These existential questions deepened in their tone as our country's political and racial landscapes shifted like tectonic plates under our feet, cracking open ground we thought was secure, exposing costly vulnerabilities in our shared concept of who we were to one another. It was as though evil's thumb was pressing full force into the wounds of our collective disconnection across our many lines of difference. What had often been experienced as a persistent ache of misunderstanding unmasked itself as an open, bleeding wound in our shared skin.

When I look back on this time, I wonder, *Are there emergency rooms for our collective bodies—for our families, churches, classrooms, and workplaces—when they've reached a breaking point? Where do we go when we, together, need to be cared for and made whole again?*

We were about six weeks into the pandemic shutdown. I'll never forget the morning I sat down with my linen-covered monthly planner to do some scheduling for the weeks ahead. The world felt topsy-turvy, and scheduling my days gave me a sense of control, of peace. My hot coffee was sitting to my left; my pen was resting on the desk to my right. I began turning the pages in my planner, taking note of all the activities I would need to remove because of lockdowns and canceled events. Instead of adding new items, I pulled out my eraser and correction fluid. I began removing meetings and parties, project deadlines and work gatherings. Blank space filled each page.

Months later, sitting confined in an emergency room hospital bed felt strangely similar to sitting at my desk with an empty calendar. Both situations forced me to have a confrontation with reality: *I have limits, and I cannot control the world.* In that confrontation, I had a choice. I could force myself to move forward as though nothing were different and as though nothing truly needed to change, or I could surrender to my limits and enter the vulnerable and challenging work of embracing slow time.

Beginning with Slow Time

Slow time is every moment we choose to be fully present and radically attentive to life's unfolding in the here and now. It refers to what we take in not only through our sight, sound, smell, taste, and touch but also through our emotional awareness, our spiritual sensitivity, and our willingness to look inside ourselves and be honest about what's really going on.

Slow time can be literal, meaning specific times during the day or week that we set aside to contemplate, to meditate, or to pray. Slow time can also be metaphysical and perhaps otherworldly. Author and spiritual guide Christine Valters Paintner, in her book *Sacred Time*, draws a beautiful distinction between the Greek expressions of *kronos* time and *kairos* time. *Kronos*, from which we derive the word "chronological," speaks to the daily, forward-moving, linear tick of the clock. The 1-2-3-4 . . . horizontal cadence of our days. It is the type of time we measure and the form of time to which we most often respond. *Kairos* time is an altogether different reality. *Kairos* time is those moments when heaven touches earth. It is time outside of time. It's the powerful inbreaking of new life when a baby is born into the world. It's the expansive timelessness one experiences in a cathedral during a prayerful liturgy. Kairos moments are often marked by mystery and a touch of the divine. When we enter *kairos* time, we lose sight of the forward-moving ticktock of our watches and clocks. Both *kronos* and *kairos* offer us opportunities to slow down our lives. Whether we create slow time by scheduling it (*kronos*) or we encounter slow time because heaven has touched earth (*kairos*), both are invitations to a more connected and less worried life.

It's important to know that embracing slow time isn't about feel-good days of relaxation at the beach, though I love those. It's about slowing to a pace that allows us to face reality, even when it's hard. I used to believe that "being present" meant paying attention to only the good things happening in and around me—keeping a record of the positive emotions I felt, the healthy relationships I was in, and the celebration-worthy events I experienced. While it is good and worthwhile to be attentive to all that is life-giving, author and researcher Brené Brown reminds us that we cannot selectively numb,[1] because to resist life's heartache is to resist life's joy. We cannot have one without the other. Embracing slow time is an opportunity to confront even life's most challenging realities and to meet those moments with the fullness of our attention. We'll explore how to do this in the pages to come.

Embracing slow time is like approaching a new plot for a garden. Before planting anything, we have to survey the landscape to see what *is*. What is the quality of the soil? What is the pattern of the sun moving across the sky? What weeds are growing and will need to be removed? How does the contour of the land impact the way water flows? What wildlife lives nearby and may be in relationship with whatever is grown here? Only in answering these questions can we rightly determine what seeds, trees, or types of vegetation can thrive in that particular patch of earth. Slowing down your life is carving out space to be honest about what *is* so that you can then plan for what might be.

When you let your life slow down, either by accepting the tough seasons that come your way or by intentionally carving out time for self-reflection, you make room to hear and respond to the deeper needs pulsing beneath the surface of your life. In slow moments and slow seasons, you can pay attention to and respond to your life instead of to the whims, needs, desires, and pressures from the world around you. Paying attention to your life involves making space to ask yourself, "What is going on here? What isn't working? What is driving me? What is broken here? What do I actually want?" Then you can respond with intentional, daily decisions to practice the unhurriedness you're craving. When you keep moving at a hectic, busy pace, however, rushing from one experience to another, you can get stuck in cycles of ignoring and reacting. You ignore the deeper questions because doing so seems easier and more efficient in the moment. You react from ingrained patterns of behavior that lack thoughtful intention. When you're in cycles of ignoring and reacting, you bounce around, attempting one life hack after another, hoping to feel better but never substantially altering your circumstances. Slow time invites you to get off the hamster wheel of ignoring and reacting and to welcome the margin needed to truly understand what's not working in your current approach to life and consider what needs to change for you to live in the here and now.

The idea of letting your life slow down may sound terrifying, if not completely impossible, so I want to walk you through two principles to help you imagine and eventually integrate a slower way of being into your very full and most likely very busy, daily experience. Why? So that you have the mental, emotional, spiritual, and practical margin to be radically attentive to what's right in front of you, regardless of what life brings. The two guiding principles are settling into a slower *place* and learning how to honor a slower *pace*.

On Place

Roosters were crowing in the distance. The sun was high and bright in the clearest blue sky I'd seen in ages. I rose from my bed and peered out the window, overlooking acres and acres of cattle and hayfields.

I can't believe I'm back here, I thought to myself.

My husband, Alex, and I had moved out of the city of Atlanta and into the bonus room above my parents' garage in rural middle Georgia. Our intention was to save money and then move back to the hustle, bustle, and importance of urban life. But as days turned to weeks and weeks turned to months, I began making peace with the plans the Creator had for us. I'd always sworn I would never move back to the country, but here I was, waking up to rooster crows on our family farm.

For much of my childhood, I believed I was growing up in the middle of nowhere. In no place. A point of geography belittled by virtue of being a non-city, a non-event, a non-attraction. When you come from a place that feels small, smallness runs the risk of becoming a trap, a sort of stuckness. Irrelevance and an unstated but assumed sense of worthlessness can settle in. If you're from nowhere, then surely you're no one. Or that's how it seemed to me.

Given how small, and even boring, I perceived my hometown to be, leaving "nowhere" became my prime objective. *Leave the small place; go to the big place. Leave the smallness; go be the bigness.* It made sense to me as a kid that in order to be important, I would have to break free from the tiny town and make a life in a place that made me feel important on the inside. I wanted nothing more than to disassociate from this place, from these lands, and from the slowness I equated with aimlessness and a lack of ambition. The pace of life in rural America, at least in my experience of it, was like sun-brewed tea sitting on the back porch for hours, steeping and darkening and preparing to be sweetened in time for an afternoon lunch. You couldn't rush it. It was like the thick wall of humidity that stops you in your tracks on a hot summer day in Georgia. You couldn't hurry it along. The pace of life in rural America can feel limiting and stodgy, especially if it's all you've ever known.

My sense of familiarity with the slow, small-town life is perhaps the very dynamic that positioned me to be surprised by it when we moved back. While I never intended to return to farm life, something about the way folks drove slowly through town and about the way chores took time and couldn't be rushed began to work on my soul. I also began driving more slowly. I also began attending to the chores in front of me without worry about what was next on my to-do list. Something about the slowness of the place I was living in supported me in embracing slow time. I had space in my days to sit on my parents' porch, rock in their swing, and watch the cattle graze across the fields. I was able to notice the Carolina wrens and the eastern bluebirds as they gave no thought to the calendar reminders and email notifications on my phone. I learned from the carpenter bees and the chipmunks, both wholly unbothered by the anxieties of completing to-do lists and of positioning themselves to get promoted at work. The slowness of the place, and of all the creatures in it, invited me ever more deeply into presence, into slow time.

Slow places have a non-anxious atmosphere about them. When you enter them, you can feel your heartbeat slow down and your breath deepen. It's like stepping into the living room of a dear, close friend and instantly feeling at home there. Slow places tend to be quiet, and they are places where you can hear the sounds of the natural world, whether birds chirping or leaves rustling or winds howling. Slow places make it easier for you to hear your own inner chatter because there are so few distractions in the environment around you. Slow places have a coherence and a simplicity to them.

While I found a slow place on my parents' farm, you don't have to move to a rural community to encounter the non-anxious peacefulness an environment has to offer. You can create a slow place in your home by choosing a chair, a corner, or a place on the porch dedicated to quiet and rest. You can enter a slow place by attending a liturgical service at a local church. You can find a slow place on the yoga studio floor. Anywhere you find your heartbeat slowing, your breath deepening, and your anxieties calming is a place where slowness dwells.

The slowness of a place is also tied to the relationships we have in said place. My parents' farm is a slow place for me due to both the natural environment and the love and safety my family has cultivated there over the years. You can be in a seemingly peaceful, quiet place, but if the quality of the relationships you have there is poor, you may very well not feel any peace at all. Slow places are marked both by the tranquility of the environment itself and by the relational health and connection one feels when there.

My great-uncle's stories of growing up in the rural South of the United States illustrate this beautifully. While I was living with my parents, he came to visit us on the farm one weekend. I'm always interested to learn how my relatives survived the harshness and cruelty of the Jim Crow era, so I listen to their stories closely, mining golden nuggets of wisdom that can help me survive the harshness and cruelties of our time. I asked my uncle about his experiences growing up in Georgia. He offered many tales of time spent working the land with his siblings and cousins. He told me stories of the care and connection he felt running between his home and the homes of his grandparents, aunts, and uncles. My ancestors and kin all lived within a few miles of one another and shared nearly every aspect of their daily lives. For some, there was the desire to flee north to escape the trauma of racial violence in the South, but for my uncle and many of my other relatives of his time, Georgia was home. The slowness, the heat, the gnats, and the red clay were all signposts of where they most wanted to be. "Some parts of life were hard back then," my uncle said, "but in many ways, life was better than it is now. We didn't have much, but we had each other."

As I reflect on his sharing, I'm struck by how settled, in the moment, and at home my uncle was able to feel in his life despite the violence and racial oppression he lived through. His relationships—his experience of knowing others and being known by them—nurtured a richness and a connection in a place that was also rife with harm. Slow places are not just about the environments themselves; slow places are cultivated when we nurture loving relationships in our homes, on our streets, and in our subdivisions or neighborhoods.

I had to leave the small rural community of my upbringing and return before I realized that "nowhere," in all its slowness and creation care, was actually forming a realistic pace of life within my spirit. Looking back now, I'm in awe of how lovingly "nowhere" raised me. Its freshwater creeks, gravel roads, and fields of dusty red clay were a wonderland. I'll never forget how tall I felt as I climbed a pine tree for the first time—safety and adventure all wrapped up in one grand intention as I ascended, left foot, left arm, right foot, right arm, up and up into the sky. I think of the summer days spent down at the creek, my brother and I, shoes off, following the waterway as far as we could go without fear of losing our way back home. Gathering and skipping rocks, watching tadpoles and frogs, deciding what we would do if we came across the water moccasins our father always warned us about. Those days, dripping like honey from a comb, were magical. They were the epitome of slow time, but it took me years to know it. I wonder, what physical place in your life and story has served as a portal from an untethered, disquieted existence to a more grounded and present way of being? Maybe it was a chair by a specific window in your home through which the morning light landed perfectly across the room. Maybe it was a tree in your yard, where you were able to relax into the gift of being held for a time. Maybe it was the stoop of a dear friend, where you laughed loud and full as the sun set over the skyline. Slow places can be found and made wherever you are. Where are your slow places?

On Pace

In addition to finding, cherishing, and prioritizing slow places, we can embrace slow time by integrating a slower *pace*. "Pace" refers to the speed at which we do a task or complete an activity. We live in a time when many basic activities are automated for us, which makes it easier, at least in theory, for us to get more done. Making coffee each morning is a great example. While making coffee used to require a person to grind beans, boil water, and prepare some sort of steeping and filtering mechanism, now we can wake up, pop a small plastic cup into a machine, set down our mug, and press a button. The automated coffee-making process saves us time, allowing us to attend to the other parts of our morning routine. Modern life is full of these shortcuts that, in theory, are meant to make our lives better. Instead of reading maps, we let the GPS tell us how traffic is and where to go. Instead of reading books and newspapers, we skim highlight reels on our phones. Instead of calling people or dropping by friends' houses on their birthdays, we send text messages. Instead of going to a local general store to shop for home goods, we tap our screens a few times and await the delivery. Instead of sitting across from loved ones and asking hard and good questions about their lives and days, we sit across from televisions and click through algorithmic entertainment recommendations. All these tiny automations, meant to make life better, easier, and more connected, are leaving us lonelier, more depressed, and with a lessened sense of purpose than previous generations could have imagined.

What does this have to do with embracing slow time by slowing down our pace? In my observation, all these automations disrupt our ability to lead deep and mindful lives in two ways. First, they manufacture anxiousness and distraction.

We've lost the ability to sit in quiet because we've become so accustomed to the noise. We've lost the ability to face our pain because we've become so accustomed to numbing it through technology and activity. We've lost the ability to know who we are because we've been inundated with ideas, opinions, and projections of who others think we ought to be. Automations and technological advancements overwhelm the senses and leave us feeling disjointed. We're fooling ourselves if we think they are having no effect on our bodies and souls.

Second, accumulated automations give us the impression that we are limitless. We begin to believe we are more than we are; our sense of self becomes inflated. For example, on a given day, I can reasonably accomplish one or two tasks if I'm going to do them well. However, given the ease of scheduling apps and artificial intelligence notetakers, I approach each day with the idea that if there's a blank spot in my calendar, I can and should fill it to maximize my productivity while using technology to help me do more than one thing at a time. Again, human productivity, at least for me, is doing one or two things well each day. But with technology's "help," I'm inclined to reach for much more, despite knowing that striving to do the most each day will almost always leave me feeling overextended and on the brink of burnout.

Intentionally practicing a slower pace disrupts both of these norms. Slowing down your pace will teach you how to honor the natural limitations of your personality and capacity. Practically, slowing down your pace is about finding ways to break your addiction to efficiency and to decrease your reliance on automation. Here are a few ways you might consider putting this practice to work:

- *Read poetry.* Notice how the cadence of words, commas, and line breaks compel you to stop skimming and to pay attention to each precise literary decision.

- *Take your dog (or yourself) for a walk.* If you're brave, do it without listening to a podcast or taking a phone call while you're out. Notice the light dancing in the trees overhead. Let the natural world captivate you.
- *Breathe deeply during a stressful interaction.* This will help you respond from a place of care instead of from a place of frustration.
- *Journal your thoughts.* Write with your hand instead of typing notes into your phone. Notice if you experience some inner spaciousness in the midst of whatever ideas are racing through your mind.
- *Make a pour-over coffee.* Watch as the hot water drips through the coffee beans, creating a bloom and then filtering into your favorite mug.
- *Wake up and stretch mindfully.* Moving your body with intention draws you into the present moment.

All these examples are adjustments to your *pace*, and within each of them is the opportunity to bring radical attentiveness to the here and now. Practicing slowness unfolds on multiple levels all at once. When you choose to embrace slow time in one area of your life or in one moment during the day, it *re*forms every area and every moment touched by that initial, singular, conscious choice.

As you begin to slow down, whether by entering a slow place or by integrating a habit that slows your pace, you're likely to encounter discomfort, nervousness, and frustration long before you experience any measure of peace. This resistance is normal. It's best to anticipate it so that you can move through the resistance when it comes. When considering resistance, the wisdom of renowned priest and founder of the Center for Action and Contemplation, Richard Rohr, comes to mind. There's a story in the Christian Scriptures about Jesus Christ going into the wilderness for forty days to fast and to pray. The Scriptures tell us that while he's in this time of ascetic consecration, he's met by "wild beasts."[2] Perhaps these wild beasts were literal, but in a teaching on this passage of Scripture, Rohr speaks of them metaphorically as well. When we go into our own wilderness—meaning when we slow down, stop moving, and prioritize time and space to encounter our inner lives—our own "wild beasts" tend to emerge. Our inner patterns and unsavory passions, our doubts and fears, our judgments of ourselves and others—they are all right there, looking us straight in the eye. We cannot avoid them with our busyness and our striving. Slowness becomes the doorway to true self-awareness, in all its potential goodness and its certain shame.

Embracing slow time makes room for more self-knowing than many of us are used to or comfortable with. As a result, when we first begin entering slower places and decreasing our reliance on automations and shortcuts, we're forced to really face ourselves for the first time in a long time. Facing ourselves means confronting the parts of our stories we'd rather avoid or hide. It means taking radical responsibility for how our choices are contributing to the negative outcomes we're experiencing. It means learning how to identify our needs and address our pains. It's a ton of work, so we avoid it. We keep working, or numbing, or pushing, or distracting because in the short term it's easier. But in the long term, instead of building inner strength, we're left spiraling in fearfulness and anxiety. There's another way to live, but we must learn how to move through the resistance to slow time so that we can get to the other side.

What Makes Us Resist Slow Time?

As you set out to slow down so that you can live a more grounded and present life, resistance to this change may emerge. Here are four forms of resistance you may encounter:

1. Fear of departing from the cultural norms we've inherited
2. Awareness of our responsibilities to our families and communities, which may require that we keep moving at a pace that's unsustainable
3. Uncertainty about who we are and what we're worth if we're not always achieving
4. Fear of facing the pain once we start to get really honest about what's not working

Let's take a closer look at each of these forms of resistance so we can find our way through them.

Fear of Departing from the Cultural Norms We've Inherited

For as long as I can remember, the drive to excel and to achieve has been central to my functioning in the world. I grew up in a home that often felt chaotic to my nervous system. My parents, like many, were raising kids while growing through their own challenges and trying to make their way in the world. As a military family, we moved multiple times, always in search of the right piece of land to call our own. As African American adults in the South in the early 1990s, my parents were also navigating the stress of racism prevalent in the small town we eventually settled in long term. They did their best to prepare my siblings and me for the uncertainties that exist when moving through the world in skin like ours. Together, these factors created a scenario in which performing became my refuge. Being able to go to school and eventually out into the world with an ability to excel anchored me in my body. Achievement was my safe place. I didn't know it at the time, but the hustle to make straight A's and to become president of as many high school clubs as I could was its own sort of trauma response, a reaching for certainty in an uncertain world.

In addition to the workings of my home life, I was raised by incredibly hardworking people. My parents taught me the value of doing good work with as much excellence as I could muster. One of my mother's most familiar refrains was:

> If a job is once begun, never leave it 'til it's done.
> Be the labor great or small, do it well or not at all.

We would say this poem aloud as we cleaned kitchen countertops and folded laundry. This rhyme came to mind at the outset of school projects or when taking up a new piece of music on the piano. My parents instilled within me a desire not just to complete the work in front of me but to do so with care. I was raised by folks who had to labor for every ounce of advancement they experienced, and they were diligent to knit this way of being into the fabric of our family life.

Additionally, as a young Black girl in a society where the odds were stacked against me, I learned I would have to work twice as hard as others to receive half of what others received. This way of seeing and being in the world was deeply ingrained in me, and confronting this story was and remains no small feat. For those who have stories of oppression in their background, or in the foreground of their lives, slowing down feels extremely risky because proving our place in the world seems critical to our survival. If this is your experience, I don't recommend you just throw caution to the wind and embrace slow time. Instead, practice curiosity about what is compelling you to strive in any given situation. Ask yourself, "What is driving me here? Do I need to prove myself? Or am I already more than qualified to be in this room?"

I was once sitting at a boardroom table with a group of leaders I respected and admired. I was feeling a degree of impostor syndrome as the newest and youngest addition to the room.

Next to me was seated a mentor whose coaching and support had been invaluable to me. I leaned over to her and said, "I still feel like I need to prove something to be here." She quickly, gently, and firmly said, "No. You're in the room. You're at the table. You have nothing to prove." I felt tears well up in my eyes and pushed them back with everything I could. I felt so seen and affirmed. My mentor in that moment helped me see that while I may have had to prove myself to get in the room, I did not need to keep working so hard in that particular way. I was in the room.

Shifting from living a scattered, restless life to creating a life where you feel peaceful, at home in your body, and able to receive the fullness of your life in all its forms will compel you to interrogate your cultural norms and to decide what role these norms will play going forward. If your nervous system goes awry at the prospect of slowing down because doing so goes against the cultural grain of your family's lived experience, that simply means your body is working as it should, protecting you from the unknown. Trying this new way of living will feel unsafe simply because it's new. You've never done it before. When you start to slow down, you will feel uncomfortable, on edge, and maybe even afraid.

One practice to help you move through this resistance is to speak aloud words of affirmation to yourself, especially while in a slowing down practice (i.e., self-reflection in a dedicated time and space you've set aside) or in a slowed down season (i.e., a period of time that you didn't necessarily choose but that has afforded you space for self-reflection). Here's what this looks like: When you're in a moment of embracing slow time and the anxiety, discomfort, or fear rises in your spirit, remind yourself that you're safe by literally wrapping your arms around yourself, closing your eyes if you feel comfortable doing so, taking a deep breath, and saying one of the following phrases aloud:

- I am safe.
- I am allowed to slow down.
- Slowing is safe.
- I am free to rest.
- I am okay.

You can repeat one phrase over and over again, or you can cycle through a few. You can even write your own affirmations that speak more specifically to whatever anxiety or fear you're holding.

This practice may sound too simple to be effective, but I assure you that in time your body will begin to feel at home in slowness. Moving too fast will start to feel strange. You will rewrite your narratives about hustle and striving, and the people who feel like home to you will experience the overflow of your willingness to reclaim rest and renewal.

Awareness of Our Responsibilities

Early in my process of thinking about what "a more beautiful way" could mean for the average person, I posed a prompt on Instagram to crowdsource insights on what made slow living possible or impossible. I offered this question: "What makes it difficult for you to slow down in your daily life?" Multiple people responded, but one response has lingered in my mind for years. One of my dear friends, a married mom of three young kids who also works full-time for a nonprofit in our community, said this:

> That's a great question because it's just a constant season of maintaining and sustaining. If you take time away in spurts, you're either adding that additional weight to your partner or will have to deal with it when you get back. Slow is possible if you have one avenue, like if I was just a stay-at-home mom or if I was just a full-time employee, but to do both . . . feels

> like any additional time is already taken. Guilt also feels like it diminishes the possibility for slowness. If I had a magic wand, all everyday tasks would already be taken care of, like food, shopping, dishes, clothes, and cleaning, and my mind would only have to focus on the growth of myself and my family.

She and I messaged for a while, and together we concluded that the only way slow time might be accessible for someone in shoes like hers would be for that person to live in a sort of compound in which family or community members could be true and full partners in the processes of family life.

The truth is that embracing slow time, in the practical sense of entering into slow places and moving at slower paces, may not be accessible to everyone at all times. However, I do believe my friend's reflections offer two windows into the anchoring and the attention to the moment that a more beautiful way proposes. The first window is that of community. Building relationships with others wherein it's possible to let your guard down, to ask for what you need, to share material resources, and to shoulder one another's burdens is perhaps one of the few ways those with very full lives can find a way into slow time in the technical sense—putting a block of time in the schedule for self-reflection, contemplation, and facing one's reality. I've seen people do this when they go to church and trust others to watch their kids. I've seen folks do this by hosting other families in their home and having the older kids watch the younger so the adults can have space for the questions and conversations they need. I've seen parents who have the financial resources sign up for individual or group spiritual direction sessions, which affords them a dedicated space to contemplate, to listen, and to reflect on life. There is no magic formula here, and what works for one may not work for another.

My friend's reflections also offer a second window. Embracing slow time carries the ultimate aspiration of learning how to welcome life as it is, with all its limitations and gifts, trusting that each season holds within it the exact conditions needed for growth and development at that time. The work of embracing slow time is making space, even now, to say, "This feels impossible, and yet here we are." As a person of faith, I see this as a moment to offer up a prayer or a question along the lines of "God, where are you in this? What are you up to right now? How are you meeting me here?" My desire in these moments isn't to escape reality but to become as fully engaged with reality as possible. In this way, our responsibilities cease to be hindrances to embracing slow time and become instead the very pathways we take into radical attentiveness to the reality of now. We welcome the chaos, the frustration, and the noise. We welcome the discomfort and the dis-ease. We welcome our own neediness and frailty. In time, we learn how to accept ourselves, our limits, and those around us for exactly who and what they are.

How? First, acknowledge your need for more slowness and space, and honor the reality of where you are, even if it's hard. Second, if you are able, make your need and difficulty known by sharing with friends, a therapist, a spouse, or your own soul. Remind yourself that you are not alone and that even this season will pass. If you are able to ask for help or to generate creative solutions in community, please do so, though I won't pretend such luxuries are available to everyone. Again, embracing slow time is about making room, even if only a few minutes before you get out of bed each day, to receive and accept the season you're in—even as you may be praying for the season to pass.

I'm aware that my faith and spiritual tradition profoundly shape my approach to embracing slow time in that I believe that difficulty has the potential to bring refinement and healing to the human soul. I know this isn't everyone's worldview, and you may very well see things differently than I do. But we live in a world full of challenging seasons and difficult things, and rather than destroying myself by living a numbed out and distracted life in the face of these difficulties, I have found a grace and an energy available in the moments when I surrender to what *is*. When we sit with what is on a daily basis, any decisions we make to pivot or adjust are based in reality instead of in abstraction, distraction, or fantasy. This makes all the difference. Before we can know what changes or adjustments might be possible, we have to slow down enough to be honest with ourselves and others about what's not working. In so doing, we experience greater self-knowing, and we open ourselves to the possibility of having others share their burdens with us. We get to experience the richness of being seen and known simply because we decided to slow down long enough to tell the truth.

Uncertainty About Who We Are and What We're Worth

Not a week goes by when I am not challenged by the belief that "you are only worth what you achieve and produce." Because this message is so loud in my inner life, slowing down can feel like a threat to my sense of being. Slowing down inclines me to start asking questions: Who am I if I'm not achieving? Who am I if I'm not working, advancing, progressing? Who will love me if I'm not accomplishing things for them? Who will see me if I'm not striving to be the best? Adding to this pressure is the fact that much of modern society values productivity, accomplishment, and overextending oneself, be it for the sake of money, influence, or impact. These are the waters we're swimming in. We rarely question the merit of grinding our lives down to their foundations for the sake of climbing whichever ladder we've set our sights on. This value system teaches us that as long as we're climbing higher and winning the game, it doesn't matter if our inner lives, our families, and our connections to ourselves and to one another begin to fall apart. Stepping outside this value system not only goes against the grain of culture but also stirs us up on the inside, especially if our self-value is tied to what we achieve.

For many, this intimate link between self-worth and productivity begins early in life. Given my own experience, I look on with concern when I see children praised primarily for what they accomplish instead of for their personhood and character. It is good and meaningful to praise hard work and diligence in young people; hard work and diligence are skills they'll need to survive. However, if the only time kids experience an adult's pleasure and delight in them is when they've gotten a good grade, when they've been elected for a student leadership position, or when they've made the team, we may very well create a generation of people who know how to win but have no idea who they are.

If your sense of worth and value is tied to winning, producing, and achievement, one reason you resist slowing down is because it feels threatening. If you've built your entire life and identity on reaching and maintaining a certain level of status, then slowing down can feel as if you're compromising the very ground you're standing on. If this is where you find yourself, remember there is a cost to *not* slowing down too. There is the cost of disconnection from your own heart and soul, there is the cost of disconnection from people you love, and there may also be the cost of disconnection from types of work that truly nourish you. Building an identity on what you achieve may feel energizing for a time, but it isn't an enduring foundation to sustain your life, and sustainable groundedness and connection are our aim.

In a way, slowing down does mean producing less. Producing less can *feel* like being less important, less relevant, less worthy, or less wanted. The truth, however, is that you are important, you are relevant, you are worthy, and you are wanted—whether you're achieving or not. This is another instance in which affirmations prove useful. When confronting negative beliefs related to my identity and worth, I've found the following affirmations to be helpful:

- I am loved.
- My life matters.
- I'm grateful to be here.
- I am finding my way.

If you struggle to slow down because you feel as if your worth is on the line, another practice, in addition to using affirmations, is participating in hobbies or activities simply for the fun of it. Play is an incredible antidote to the anxieties fostered by striving to earn or prove our worth. It is also a vulnerable practice in which we let our guard down, take off whatever mask we typically wear to get by, and let ourselves embrace pleasure and delight. The real challenge for the high achievers among us is to resist the temptation to turn play into another project requiring an excellent performance.

Choose a playful activity or experience and, like a child, remember what it was like to do something just for the fun of it. Doing so will help you move through the resistance to slowing down so you can build a life you're excited to live instead of one driven by obligation.

Fear of Facing the Pain

The last reason we resist embracing slow time is because we don't know what we'll do once we're face-to-face with the pain we've been running from all along. I know this feeling all too well. We keep running in hopes that the monsters in our closets never catch up to us. When this happens, however, the pain we're avoiding becomes the driving force of our lives, even if it's out of view. Pain from our childhoods, pain created by our own choices, pain in our relationships with others, and even physical pain in our bodies—our lives have a way of forming around pain's priorities instead of around the intentional decisions we make for ourselves. Over time, it becomes easier to pretend we're fine and to just keep moving. This isn't sustainable though. Whether we choose to create slow time because we're exhausted by life or slow time shows up on our doorstep due to circumstances we didn't see coming, the only way forward is *through* the pain.

How people face pain varies, but there are a few postures you can adopt to hold yourself and your pain lovingly and with care. A first posture is one of honest acknowledgment. You have to acknowledge the pain is there. Pain can be great at hiding, especially underneath emotions like anxiety and resentment, or underneath actions like overworking or substance abuse. It can take some time for you to get honest with yourself about where pain is lurking in the shadows, often masked by an emotion or behavior. Acknowledging your pain simply by noting to yourself that it's there is the beginning of facing it directly.

A second posture is one of open-mindedness, wherein you face your pain with curiosity instead of judgment or shame. Judgment ends the conversation; curiosity opens the conversation. The more open and curious you can be about the pain you're experiencing, about where it's coming from, about what it's in response to, and about the needs it's advocating for, the more precise and effective your healing process can be. You can apply the right medicine only if you know exactly what needs healing.

A third posture to adopt when facing your pain is one of gentleness. Emotional pain, not unlike physical pain, is tender to the touch. Applying pressure or moving too fast can cause more harm than good. You want to hold your pain, and yourself, gently and with care. This looks like not rushing. This looks like sharing your pain with people who feel truly safe. This looks like wrapping yourself in love by drinking enough water, eating nourishing meals, and prioritizing laughter and play. This looks like resisting any pressure you feel to be perfect, to move on quickly, or to hide in fear and shame. Gentleness protects the most vulnerable parts of you while guiding you toward restoration.

Processing pain is not work we can typically do our own. While we can work out some things through practices like journaling and prayer, the heaviest lifting happens in the context of relationship. What I find most hopeful is that not a single person on the earth escapes pain. It is truly a universal human experience, meaning you are not alone in your need for support, advocacy, and safety.

If you start to slow down your life in the ways outlined in this chapter, you will likely bump into pain that needs your attention. It will not devour you. It will not destroy you. But it does need to be named, witnessed, held, grieved, and then integrated into the story of who you're becoming. I've found therapy and counseling to be vital. I've found intentional conversations with two or three trusted friends to be essential. I've found journaling and pouring out my heart on paper to be critically important. All these practices can help you attend to the pain that greets you as you start to embrace slowing down.

Slowing Down Is Just the Beginning

Brave work has gotten you here. Choosing to wake up to the reality of your life and to the anxiety, dread, and scatteredness you've been feeling is no small task. Choosing to slow down by creating intentional space or by surrendering to the slowness that has found its way to you is courageous work. Resistance will pop up, as it does whenever we set out to change something, but know that through affirmations, surrender, playfulness, and a willingness to face the pain in your own story, you will find your way to the other side.

Slowing down is just the beginning. We have good work to do in attending to our bodies and souls in the pages to come. Before moving forward, I encourage you to create some slow time right now.

What are you feeling? Emotionally? Sensationally?

What is stirring for you as you consider the invitations offered in this chapter?

Take a deep breath.

And another.

And another.

You are doing brave work. You are learning to live a more beautiful way.

Two

CONNECTING WITH YOUR BODY

I lay on the firm grassy earth, held safely underneath the periwinkle and baby-pink cotton candy sky. The sunset was calming, blanketed over me like a hand-sewn quilt made by my mother. I was tucked into the Arizona desert—fully aware, fully content, more at home in my body than I had felt in years. My eyes traced the edge of one of the mountains standing off in the distance. There it was, shaped like a rough-hewn arrowhead, red and proud and pointing to the heavens.

My fingers moved gently as I brushed them back and forth across my torso, two inches below my belly button, right where the fibroids used to be. They were gone now. The surgery table made it so. But my body remembered. As my hands moved back and forth, tenderly and with care, I contemplated all my womb had been through. I contemplated the struggle and strain of nights spent on the edge of life, of hemorrhaging from the inside out. I contemplated the emergency room visits, the blood transfusions, the doctor's exclamation, "I can't even believe you're standing right now."

I lay on the earth, underneath the desert sky, at ease and relieved to be free of the unwanted growths that had rendered my body weak and empty. It had been months since my surgery, and I decided to go on this retreat in the desert because, while my physical body was recovering, my emotional and spiritual health needed nourishment and care. The surgery freed me from the massive growths in my uterus, but freedom from what ailed me is not the same as the presence of well-being, connectedness, and wholeness. I wanted to be whole.

Embracing slow time is the beginning of the journey to a more beautiful way to live. Slowness, presence, and attentiveness to the here and now are what make room for us to see ourselves and our lives with clear and honest eyes. As we settle into slow time, we turn our attention to the body. Our bodies carry tremendous wisdom about what makes for a firmly established and unhurried life. We experience peace in our bodies. We feel whether or not we have energy in our bodies. We express our values and needs through our bodies. A more beautiful way to live is not an intellectual exercise. It is a way of being that is expressed in these bodies, in our very skin.

In the coming pages, we'll first explore what disconnection from our bodies is like and some of the reasons we experience this disconnection in the first place. Then we'll discuss what connection to our bodies (or "embodiment") is, why it matters, and how we can nurture restorative and healing connection with our bodies.

On Being Deeply Disconnected

In the season leading up to my visit to the emergency room, my everyday life was not unlike the everyday lives of most people

I knew. I woke up early, prepared for the day, drove to work, performed at work, drove home, spent time with my family, went to sleep, and did it all again. Life was busy, active, and full. There were parts of my life that I loved dearly: the purposeful work, the relationships with friends, the satisfaction of bringing meaningful creations to life. There were also parts of my life that I didn't love—namely, the anxiety and the persistent sense that the pace of my days was going to drown me.

When indications that my body was unwell initially began to surface, I thought very little of them. *This will pass soon*, I told myself. *I'll keep pushing through*. Pushing through pain. Pushing through skipped meals. Pushing through anxiety. Pushing through fear. Eventually, all the pushing birthed symptoms I couldn't ignore. There were sleepless nights, life-halting menstrual cycles, a consistently high heart rate, and shortness of breath in situations where I should have been able to breathe just fine.

Being unwell in one's body is not special or remarkable. It is a common, daily, very human experience. Being regularly unwell, however, and moving too fast and pushing so hard that you don't even notice how much care your body is crying out for? Well, that's a different reality altogether. I knew I was out of balance, but I didn't yet understand that my body was asking me to make major changes. I simply concluded that the problem must be me; I just couldn't seem to perform as well as everyone else. My mind ended up in a loop of questions: Why can't I keep up? Why am I not enjoying the busyness and intensity of this lifestyle like everyone else? Why do I need so much coffee to be ramped up and focused? What is wrong with me?

This barrage of inner critiques led to a less-than-helpful game plan: *Maybe I need to work out more. Maybe I need to organize my schedule better. Maybe I'm not asking for enough help.* The list went on and on, little tweaks here and there, all in an effort to force my body to follow the pace of the world around me. It's frustrating to feel as if your body and its limitations are preventing you from keeping up with all you're told you're supposed to be and do. My body became unwell because I was forcing it to maintain an ill-fitting pace and standard of productivity. This way of relating to myself, to my own body, made me feel tremendously disconnected, meaning there was a breakdown in communication between my body's felt needs and my conscious action to respond to those needs.

Being disconnected from our bodies can look like any number of things. When I was in my most intense seasons of work, I often moved so quickly and relied so heavily on adrenaline and caffeine that I rarely heard my body's hunger. I suppressed this basic need and became undernourished, which exacerbated the stress and anxiety I was experiencing. I had a racing heartbeat and aches and pains that I did my best to set aside. Our bodies can be doing their best to send us warning signals, but when we get so used to ignoring these signals, we don't give our bodies the care they truly need. This is not to say that every bodily need or limitation is a problem to be solved; our bodies are complicated. This is to say, however, that our bodies do speak messages to us through their tensions, changes, and pains, communicating with our hearts and minds. But if we are disconnected from our bodies, we miss out on the wisdom and direction they have to offer.

How We Become Disconnected

There are many reasons we disconnect from our bodies. In those moments, it's as though our conscious minds are in one place while our physical bodies are in another, having two completely different experiences. Some of the reasons for this disconnection are personal, while others are cultural and religious.

Personal Causes

I was once watching a historical fiction television show in which a woman experienced a sexual assault. I tend to fast-forward through scenes of violence because I find them overwhelming, but this show took an approach to telling the story that surprised me. Instead of depicting the violent harm unfolding in the scene, the show depicted the woman's mental escape to another time and place. It showed us, the viewers, where her mind went, instead of keeping us locked in to what was happening for the character in real time. This way of telling the story has stayed with me for years because it so powerfully illustrated how our minds and bodies work together to keep us safe, even if it means our minds and our bodies have to go their separate ways at certain times.

Experiences of trauma, abuse, assault, or physical harm often lead to disconnection. When we experience the truly horrible, our incredibly well-designed bodies help us get through the harm by facilitating a sort of mental escape. Our minds go to a different place altogether so that we can survive what is happening. Experts call this "dissociation."[1] We leave our selves behind to get to the other side of the worst life has to offer us.

We also disconnect from our bodies because we've internalized messages that tell us to do so. In a culture that values productivity above all else, honoring the pace and needs of our bodies can feel like a luxury or a distraction from "working hard." One of the loudest myths I tend to believe is "You are lazy if you let yourself rest." *Lazy*. The word lands like a weight on my chest, leaving me feeling horrible about being human. There are other messages too, like "Only the privileged get to take care of their bodies," "Being connected with your body is a waste of precious time," and "Taking care of your body is too expensive." These internalized messages make us resistant to embracing the very things our bodies need most: loving attention, stewardship, and care.

Cultural Causes

Disconnection from our bodies flows not only from our personal encounters with traumatic events and negative internalized messages but also from age-old cultural ideas about what it means to be an evolving, advancing human. We live with the many downstream effects of the Enlightenment, the seventeenth- and eighteenth-century philosophical and intellectual movement that underpinned many of the political, industrial, and scientific revolutions that ushered in the world as we know it today.[2] Enlightenment ideals value rationality, logic, and reason over the body's innate wisdom, stories, and experiences. Through this way of seeing, we learn to make much of the scientific and to diminish both the bodily and the mystical. We are taught to elevate what can be known by way of measurement and calculation and to devalue what can be known by way of intuition and spirit. This way of thinking fractures how humans are designed—as bodies with thinking minds, feeling hearts, discerning spirits, and various abilities to form and be formed by the world.

Bodies become objects in an Enlightenment frame of mind. The earth's body becomes a resource to be privatized, bartered, traded, and sold, and from which we can extract perceived value at will. Our bodies and the bodies of others become objects too, mere vehicles for implementing the mind's vision, no matter the cost. Enslavement is possible only when some bodies are believed to be merely as worthy as their output for the greater machine. Genocide is possible only when some bodies are believed to be distractions from the larger aim of progress, rendering them disposable. This is to say very little about the cultural erasure—the lost languages, the lost medicines, the lost treks, the lost songs, the lost names for the divine—that must be grieved because certain things were deemed "irrational," "illogical," or "unreasonable." We forget what it means to be human, storied people when we lose our connection to our bodies, to our respective indigeneity, and to the body of the earth from which we came. Disembodiment is disconnection from who we are, from one another, and from the created world.

Religious Causes

Religious traditions have complex and at times conflicting views on the human body. On the one hand, the body is to be distrusted, resisted, and controlled. The body is evil, sinful, and even dirty. On the other hand, the body is to be protected, covered up, and held in modesty as a paragon of virtue. It's confusing to hold such divergent views about oneself, about one's impulses, desires, and needs. Our relationships with our bodies can be deeply disoriented by the religious contexts of our upbringing. If you're raised to believe your body is dirty, evil, and the fount of no good thing, then dissociation becomes a means of surviving the pain and shame of being a body at all.

These varied causes of disconnection do not unfold in isolation. The personal, cultural, and religious drivers of disconnection from our bodies work on us all at once, compounding the reasons we may experience and remain in a state of disconnection. Being a body is not always easy. I've known seasons when it felt as though my body was working against me, keeping me from being able to live the life I'd dreamed of, and it became challenging to believe my body had anything wise or good to offer. Beyond my own experience, there are the disabilities that society seems to have no room for. There are the diseases for which there seems to be no cure. There are the infertilities that drag people through torrential waves of disappointment and grief. There are the losses, the changes, the aging, the growth. Bodily contentment and self-acceptance are hard to come by when there is no shortage of surgeries, makeup, and clothes to make us look like anything and anyone other than who we are. When we feel as though our bodies do not fit for one reason or another, we begin to feel unsafe or as if our bodies are a liability. Disconnecting, again, becomes the way we stay alive.

Thankfully, while the causes of disconnection are plenty, so are our opportunities to restore our connections with our bodies and to bring restoration to what's often felt as a mind-body divide.

Embodiment as Connection

The best word I know to describe connection with the body is "embodiment." Embodiment is feeling connected with and at home in one's flesh.[3] It is sensual, textured, and concrete. I'm talking about the hands holding this book, the rise and fall of your lungs as you breathe, any tension you're feeling in your frame as you move through these pages. Embodied living involves our actual flesh and bones. Embodiment invites us to unlearn the tendency to brush off our felt bodily needs and to instead center our bodies as sites of wisdom and direction.

Becoming embodied is a process of listening to the vessel holding your life. This work is important because as long as you remain disconnected, you'll feel untethered and unable to experience the safety and nourishment of being rooted, which is foundational to leading a less scattered, less anxious, and less fearful life. We are made for connection with ourselves, with the earth, and with each other. Embodiment is what equips and empowers us to make real choices in the real world, choices that lead to not only our own well-being but also the well-being of those around us.

Embodiment is a practice we *do* and not merely an idea we think about. Therefore, the best way to understand this work of connection with our bodies is to recognize *how* we do it.

How We Become (Re)Connected

You must begin with the awareness that you are a body. Clinical psychologist and researcher Dr. Hillary McBride, in her book *The Wisdom of Your Body*, says, "The body is not something you have but something you are."[4] Your body is not a mere vehicle to carry your insides through the world. Your body is you. Your body knows wisdom. Your body holds your life. Your body's needs, flutters, limitations, and gifts are all invitations and guides.

Once you have an awareness that you are a body, the next step is to practice listening to your body. Listening to your body means slowing down enough to check in with your physical self about what you need or about how your body is feeling in any given moment. A way to do this is through a body scan. Lie down or sit upright in a chair and close your eyes. After you're comfortably settled, bring your attention to each part of your body, progressively scanning from the bottom of your feet all the way to the crown of your head. As you move up—from toes to feet to ankles to shins to knees—see what you notice in each part of your body. Is there tension or discomfort? Are there tingles or sensations? Is there tightness or ease? Simply notice. Begin to listen to your body. In these first few steps, your goal is to cultivate awareness. You don't have to begin meeting all the needs right away. You are building a muscle of attention, and in so doing, you are reweaving the connection between your conscious mind and your body. Connection is the goal.

Learning how to honor the needs and limits of my body, especially during recovery from surgery and burnout, required daily practice. In the initial days of my recovery, I remember waking up, keeping my eyes closed, taking a deep breath, and asking my body, "What do you need right now?" What amazed me, again and again, was how often my body would respond: "I need a walk," "I need water," "I need sunlight," "I need a hug." Even now, many years later, I still check in throughout the day with the same question, and my body knows its needs without fail. It is up to me to listen.

Practices like the body scan help us connect with our bodies by teaching us how to listen to and notice what our bodies are trying to say. Here are a few examples of body signals I've gathered from my own life and from friends:

- A tight jaw signals stress or an inability to say what you want to say.
- Persistent digestive issues signal that you've been avoiding difficult conversations or resisting challenging emotions.
- Eye twitches signal too much time on screens and result from the anxiety the screens generate.
- Slumped or tight shoulders signal sadness, disappointment, or despair.
- Headaches signal an excess of rumination or worry.
- Lower back pain signals a potential need for greater relational support in life.
- A higher than normal resting heart rate signals a need for food, water, or a break from a stressful mental activity.

This list is not exhaustive, and a body scan is not a perfect science. What I'm aiming to convey is that our bodies are having holistic experiences. Our thoughts and emotions and stressors impact our physical forms and vice versa. As you chart what it looks like for you to integrate more mindfulness in your daily life, I'm confident that your body will teach you what a more beautiful way uniquely means for you.

In addition to performing a body scan, connection with your body can be facilitated through somatic, or body-based, healing modalities. These are especially helpful to recover a sense of safety after experiencing trauma or harm. One such modality is conscious breathwork, in which a facilitator guides you through a series of breathing exercises that relieve stress, increase focus, and even open a pathway for emotional release. I've experienced all of the above in facilitated breathwork sessions and have walked away feeling safer and more at home in my skin than ever before. An experienced breathwork or somatic coach can teach you how to breathe, stretch, dance, and move your body in ways that will deepen your embodiment practice. I have found somatic work to be especially effective at addressing past body-based traumas. Transformation happens as we change what we *do*, not just what and how we think.

As you seek to leave behind a life that feels overwhelming and out of control, your body's wisdom will be one of your most trustworthy guides. Your body often knows when you're living beyond your capacity long before your mind does. Your body knows when you feel unsafe long before your brain catches up to reality. The way you feel in your skin is perhaps the truest compass you'll ever have. This doesn't mean you let your bodily sensations make all your decisions for you. That would lead to impulsivity and could create more chaos than peace. The invitation here is to give your body a seat at the table, to include its wisdom in your council of life advisers, to take seriously its nudges, insights, and needs. Your body's wisdom is a gift. Ignoring, dismissing, and disregarding your body will undermine every dream you set your sights on. Connecting with, listening to, and honoring your body will leave you feeling more whole and at home in your life.

When Connection Feels Challenging

Much like with embracing slow time, listening to your body doesn't guarantee that you'll arrive at a satisfying and nourishing place right away. If you've lived disconnected from your body for a long time, the work of reconnection may very well feel worse before it feels better. Getting to the roots of why the disconnection is there in the first place can be challenging or even painful. I want to offer a couple of suggestions as you begin the task of reconnecting with your body.

First, be honest with yourself. If disconnection from your body was truly working for you, you wouldn't be reading this book. You're here, I'm guessing, because you're wondering if another way is possible. I'm here to tell you that, yes, another way is possible, but it will cost you your current way of doing life. I cannot guarantee sunshine and rainbows; life doesn't work that way. I can assure you, however, that coming home to your body will build a resilience and a capacity in you that will strengthen the core of your life so you can withstand whatever storms come your way. I know this to be true.

So interrogate your current narrative about your body and about what it means to care for your body. For example, if you believe that slowing down to listen to the needs of your body is a luxury, ask yourself where that belief comes from. Get curious about it. Who told you this? What taught you this? How is this belief serving you? You can do this interrogation in your mind, or you can go the extra mile and write in your journal. Once you've examined your current narrative, you can decide whether to hold on to that narrative or let it go. If you choose to let it go, it's important that you make an exchange, replacing the old belief with a new one. A new belief might be "My body is important and worthy of care and attention." Interrogating old belief patterns and replacing them with new ones empowers you to take ownership of the life you're creating and the story you're telling. Disempowerment, or a lack of agency over one's body and choices, is often one of the most challenging aspects of having experienced a trauma or harm that compelled you to disconnect from your body in the first place. Choosing how you will listen and relate to the precious gift of your body is one of the most healing and beautiful aspects of facing the pain of your past and moving toward a capable and resilient future.

My second suggestion comes from my faith tradition, and it is to meditate on the inherent goodness of being a body. This can be a challenging but profound shift in how you think about yourself and the material world. In the Christian tradition, we dwell within the mystery of God made flesh, of holy incarnation. In this mystery, the Creator took on the full form of creation and in so doing conferred tremendous value on the experience of embodiment. This mystical reality also conferred tremendous value on the created world: the dust, the clay, the mountains, the waters, the hills. They all sing of divine goodness and glory. I believe that when we give ourselves to the good work of weaving a connection between our minds, bodies, and souls, we enter into a truly sacred dance with the divine. The practice of embodiment is not just about our personal healing. In a small way, our individual healing is a depiction of the sort of renewal that we hope is possible throughout all of creation.

The Journey Continues

So far on this journey of living a more beautiful way, we've embraced slow time. We've practiced connecting with and listening to our bodies. Before we move ahead, you're invited to do a quick body scan.

Settle your body. Close your eyes. Begin at your feet and progressively move to the crown of your head. No need to rush. Take your time.

What do you notice?

How are you feeling?

What does your body need?

After listening to your body and responding to any needs that arise, it's time to go within and consider what it means to awaken to your inner terrain.

Three

AWAKENING TO YOUR INNER TERRAIN

The room was empty, but the warmth of the morning sunlight poured in through the south-facing window. Rays of light bounced all around the off-white walls, painting the space with a brightness, warmth, and care my soul desperately needed. I'd woken up, eaten breakfast, gotten dressed—the usual. It was a day like most any other day, but I was unemployed now and grieving. Uncertainty weighed heavily on my chest as my mind raced between regret about the past and fears about the future. Life had brought me to this moment of slow time, an opportunity to be fully present and radically attentive to the heartache right in front of me. Since I was no longer working hectic hours, even my body had begun settling into this new pace of life. No more running. No more distractions. It was time to face myself.

I gathered my supplies: a spiral-bound notebook with dot grid pages and a hunter-green cover, a Japanese gel pen with a .38 fine point, and a cushion for sitting on the floor. Sitting on the floor anchored me as the weight of my body found rest and support in the firmness of the earth. I struck a match and lit a candle, the flame serving as a gentle reminder: *Bethaney, God is here. You are not alone.*

I sat and I wrote for hours. I prayed. I wept. After months and months of moving so quickly that I'd nearly forgotten my own name, returning to my inner life in this moment of reflection was like coming home to an overgrown, unkept yard full of disorder and debris. I'd been so focused on tending to the gardens of the world, to the needs and production and cultivation of others, that my own garden—my own inner life—was in desperate need of tending and care. This moment of processing my thoughts and emotions by spilling them onto the pages of my journal was the beginning of many more moments in which I began to grapple with the singular challenging reality that there are only two gardeners who can truly steward the inner terrain of one's life: the One who created it and the one to whom it belongs. For much too long, I outsourced my sense of inner well-being to those around me. I looked to my loved ones, my mentors, my spiritual teachers, and my community to tell me who I was and what my life should be about. While there is a time and place to be influenced and shaped by others, being so externally focused and relying heavily on external validation had left my inner life in utter disarray. I didn't know who I was. I didn't know what I was about. I'd been moving too fast and doing too much to even ask these questions. This moment of confrontation—sitting on my bedroom floor and processing all that had unfolded in the months prior—helped me see that the only way I could leave a fearful, rootless, and distracted way of life behind was if I, in partnership with the divine, took responsibility for the landscape of my inner world.

Embracing slow time and connecting with our bodies so that we can listen to and learn from their wisdom are the two practices that lay a foundation for us to turn inward. This is where we begin the challenging, fruitful work of stewarding our inner lives. Living in a way that feels settled, alive to right now, receptive and accepting, requires that we become skilled gardeners who lovingly tend to our souls. For people of faith, this is very much spiritual work. If faith is not your orientation, the practices of self-reflection and self-tending remain open and available to you.

Self-reflection, when done alone or in prayerful relationship with the divine, is the practice of holding up a mirror to one's life and story and making meaning there. While self-reflection is often overlooked or dismissed as too self-focused or self-centered, effective and sincere self-reflection remain foundational to accessing our agency as people and to creating healthy relationships with those around us. Self-reflection is the pathway by which we integrate and metabolize the many lessons that life teaches. When the world is spinning and reality feels just beyond the realm of what we can influence and change, self-reflection is the ever-present invitation to focus on what we can influence, cultivate, and control. This is the work of tending to one's inner terrain.

Defining the Inner Terrain

The inner terrain is the sacred and holy place within each of us from which the materiality of each life flows. It is the place within from which we speak. It holds the dreams, desires, and deep needs of our hearts. It's where we keep our secrets, our fears, our heartbreaks, and our resentments. It's where we contemplate our biggest decisions and ask life's most consequential questions. It's the place we meet the divine. It's also the place we meet ourselves. The inner terrain is not quite the same as the mind, which is often full of thoughts and ideas, moving quickly and processing information. The inner terrain is perhaps most closely likened to the soul, to that eternal spark of being residing within us and from which we derive the animating energies that make us alive.

I refer to this as an "inner" terrain because it's a hidden place on the inside. No one can see or touch it. It's mysterious and inaccessible to the five senses. Author and teacher Parker J. Palmer, when speaking of this inner terrain, or the soul, likens it to an animal in the woods. He says, "The soul is like a wild animal—tough, resilient, savvy, self-sufficient and yet exceedingly shy. If we want to see a wild animal, the last thing we should do is to go crashing through the woods, shouting for the creature to come out. But if we are willing to walk quietly into the woods and sit silently for an hour or two at the base of a tree, the creature we are waiting for may well emerge, and out of the corner of an eye we will catch a glimpse of the precious wildness we seek."[1]

"Terrain" simply means *ground*. Ground, as a metaphor, holds multiple helpful images for us. We stand on the ground. We plant seeds in the ground. The ground requires nourishment. The ground grows vegetation. The ground needs tending. Our souls, or inner lives, function in much the same way. We stand on the values and dreams we hold. We plant thoughts, words, ideas, and possibilities like seeds in this inner place. Our inner lives require nourishment, love, and care. Our inner lives bear fruit and require tending. Awakening to your inner terrain is about getting into the soil of your life and making decisions about who you want to be from the inside out.

Becoming familiar with your inner terrain, or getting familiar with the landscape of your inner life, is not to be confused with self-obsession. Self-obsession is what happens when you become consumed with your own thoughts, feelings, and needs to the detriment of your relationships with others and your relationship with the world around you. It is not to be confused with worry and fruitless rumination, which is when your brain's negative thoughts or emotional patterns get stuck in one place—like a record that skips, repeating the same lines over and over again. The end of both self-obsession and rumination is isolation, which is how you know you're not living a life of groundedness, presence, and connection. Becoming familiar with your inner terrain is about cultivating constructive self-knowledge. It is the work of simply knowing yourself—your limitations, your hang-ups, your gifts, and your needs. When you know yourself, you are able to communicate who you are and what you value, and you are empowered to make informed decisions about the life you want to create.

There are a couple ways to come back to healthy self-knowledge if you find yourself on a path of isolation by way of self-obsession or rumination. One way is to invite a trusted friend or therapist into your inner world for a time. You can do this by letting them read a few pages from your journal or by sharing with them what you're learning about yourself and asking them to share their reflections with you. By opening up the conversation, you're still getting to know your inner terrain, but you're not doing it alone.

A few years ago, I was in deep need of someone to help me process what was stirring in my inner world. I had been working as a racial equity facilitator and had reached a point of disillusionment in my work. I no longer believed the theories I'd built my practice on. My clients were much slower to make changes in their organizations than I thought they'd be. I was bored with teaching the same workshops and giving the same talks, and I was confused about what all this meant for my life, my work, my consulting practice, and my income. I'd done my best to journal my thoughts, but I still felt stuck, alone, and isolated. I couldn't seem to generate any new ideas or creative options. I was trapped in either-or, black-and-white thinking. There was no nuance, no creativity, no gray. I knew nothing good or helpful would come from such a dire and lonely place unless I invited someone in to help me make sense of it all.

I reached out to a spiritual director, a person whose job is to accompany others as they navigate the inner terrain of their lives. My spiritual director listened to me as I turned my thoughts, feelings, and intuitive nudges over in my spirit. She asked me pointed and thoughtful questions. Through her curiosity, attentiveness, and care, she helped me weave together the threads of what mattered most to me in that season. Through our sessions, I came to a point of clarity about my values and about what needed to change in my life so I could facilitate greater alignment with what mattered most to me. This was good work that I could not do on my own.

A second way to avoid the trappings of self-obsession or the fruitlessness of rumination is to lean into connection with something greater than yourself. As a person of faith, I grow my familiarity with my inner terrain by nurturing my understanding of the nature of God through spiritual community, by reading the Christian Scriptures, and through a regular practice of prayer. When I'm tempted to begin navel-gazing, it's as though the divine prompts me to lift my eyes. David G. Benner, in his book *The Gift of Being Yourself: The Sacred Call to Self-Discovery*, says it this way: "Self-knowledge that is pursued apart from knowing our identity in relationship to God easily leads to self-inflation. . . . It can also lead to self-preoccupation. Unless we spend as much time looking at God as we spend looking at our self, our knowing of our self will simply draw us further and further into an abyss of self-fixation."[2]

To be caught up in self-reflection and self-knowing apart from something bigger than yourself is to linger in shallow waters. Your self-knowledge deepens when you open up your story to others. When done well, knowing your inner terrain leads not to isolation but to stronger relationships and more enriching service to the world around you. Why? Because when you know who you are, you are able to make decisions that enhance your life instead of ones that lead you into further anxiety, fear, and disconnection. Getting to know the lay of the land within yourself is one of the most empowering things you can do to create a non-anxious life.

Why Your Inner Terrain Matters

Let's think of the contents of your inner terrain in terms of fractals. Derived from the Latin *fract-*, which means "broken,"[3] a fractal is a geometric shape in which patterns at a small scale are similar to those at a larger scale. "Each part . . . has the same statistical character of the whole."[4] The natural world is filled with them, these tiny reminders that what makes up the smallest expression of a fern leaf or tree branch or pine cone or snowflake is the same pattern, repeated over and over again, that makes up the whole.

What if the fractal nature of anxiety in my inner life plays a role in the broader culture of anxiety I live in? What if the fractal nature of my drive to prove my worth is in some way connected with modern society's addiction to hustle culture? What if any hatred or resentment I harbor toward my neighbor is, fractally, the same hatred or resentment I see spewing across my country's political landscape? I don't draw these connections to produce blame. Quite the opposite actually. If the texture of our inner lives, when scaled up, has the potential to cause destruction, then surely the same creative capacity exists to cultivate beauty, peace, support, and care. Surely we can tend to our inner lives in such a way that, as with fern leaves and tree branches and pine cones and snowflakes, when scaled up across a family, town, country, or world, they foster tremendous good. Perhaps daily devotion to the cultivation of our inner terrains is, on some level, world-changing activity. Perhaps the work of slowing down, tending to our bodies, confronting all the broken and beautiful growing inside us, and then making choices about who we want to be is in fact revolutionary.

In practice, awakening to your inner terrain and stewarding what you discover there involves taking responsibility for how what's happening inside you is shaping the world outside you. This work of self-awareness, reflection, and responsibility is not about trying to manifest, manipulate, or control reality. It is about turning inward and attending to what's inside so that you can turn outward with clarity and intention. It is about reclaiming your power and attention from the many voices and noises clamoring for your gaze so that you can make proactive decisions about how to steward your time, your energy, and your resources. It is also about being diligent to take care of your own soul, to address any heartbreak, resentment, or disappointment you're carrying so that your experiences of pain can be integrated into your story and cease to be in the driver's seat of your life.

In 1997, author Stephen Covey coined a framework that helps people take this type of responsibility for their inner life. When I was first introduced to this framework, it transformed my understanding of what it looks like to live in an empowered and proactive way. The framework is called the "Circle of Influence."[5] In this framework, Covey distinguishes between people who are reactive and people who are proactive. Reactive people are those whose primary focus and attention are on what is outside the realm of their influence or their ability to make a difference. They are directed and pulled at by all that concerns them, despite their relative inability to do something about what's filling their hearts and minds. Here is a list of potential concerns any one of us might have on any given day:

- decisions made by world leaders about war, trade, or the economy
- wardrobe selections made by a friend prior to a group activity

- presentation topics chosen by our boss for a big event
- any number of world events that pop up on our social media feeds
- the emotional immaturity displayed by a family member at a recent holiday celebration

It's normal to be concerned about any number of things in life. They prick our hearts, fill our minds, and weigh heavily on our souls. What Covey points out, however, is that being consumed by what concerns us places us in a posture of ongoing reactivity, especially when what's concerning us is outside our control. We cannot control the decisions world leaders make about war, trade, or the economy. We cannot control what our friends choose to wear. We cannot control our boss's decisions. We cannot control what people post on their social media feeds, nor can we control the emotional immaturity of those we love. These situations and dynamics may concern us, and some of them should, but we are limited in our ability to change them. Remaining fixated on what is outside our control diminishes our ability to meaningfully steward the resources we do have.

Proactive people, in contrast, are those whose primary focus and attention are on what is inside their realm of influence. Proactive people are focused on the people, places, stories, emotions, ideas, and habits that are within their ability to change. Proactive people are powerful because they direct their efforts toward not just what matters to them but where they can have the greatest impact. Here's how a proactive person might think about the various concerns listed above:

- I can't control the decisions world leaders make, but I can vote, talk with loved ones about the issues that matter to me, protest and march, and make my voice heard in my community.

- My friend is free to make decisions related to clothing, fashion, and self-expression.
- I may not be able to change what my boss chooses to present at a work event, but I can find ways to make recommendations that move the team toward its goals.
- I can unfollow voices online that generate anxiety, set boundaries with social media, and amplify messages that are most important to me.
- I cannot control a loved one's emotional immaturity, but I can take responsibility for my own emotions, my own words, and my own boundaries and choices.

Within this framework, your inner terrain is your circle of influence. It is *yours*. When you make stewarding your inner life a priority, you situate yourself in a truly powerful position. One reason we end up feeling disquieted and consternated in our lives is because we find ourselves in reactive positions. This can be due to our choices, circumstances we didn't choose, or a combination of both. Being in a continually reactive state drains our energy, siphons off our creativity, and leaves us feeling empty. While many of us can survive in this state during crisis situations or especially challenging seasons, reactivity is not a firm foundation on which to build a life. Being proactive, however, and taking responsibility for what we can control have a positive cascading effect. They build momentum and confidence. There's nothing quite like learning how to ask, in the most difficult situations, "Even in this, what can I do?" Being proactive is not a recipe for a conflict-free life, but it is a practice that will help you build strength and resiliency so you can stand in the face of whatever comes your way.

Awakening to What's Going on Inside

Our aim at this stage in the process of living a more beautiful way is simply to become aware. One of my most cherished practices for increasing our awareness of what's going on inside our souls is the prayer of examen. The word "examen" is from the Latin *exigere*, which means "to weigh accurately." Made famous by St. Ignatius of Loyola, the prayer of examen allows a person to examine their day, look for signposts of divine presence, and ask for guidance. What I appreciate about this prayer is that it's accessible to both those of us who come from a faith tradition and those of us who do not. This prayer is not a collection of words you say; it is a process of self-reflection.

Within the prayer are two primary themes: consolation and desolation. Consolation refers to those moments, sensations, and experiences that lift your soul. They are the experiences that bring you joy, insight, satisfaction, and delight. They give you energy and spark your joy. Even challenging experiences can be considered consolations if you know them to be moments in which good pressure was created, lessons were learned, or much-needed growth happened. Consolations are experiences that you know are adding meaning, purpose, and value to your life. Desolation refers to moments and experiences that drain you. They weigh heavily on your spirit. They feel like disconnection, perhaps even isolation. They are moments when you feel brought low and as if you're carrying the weight of the world all on your own. Desolations are those experiences that seem to take more than they give, and they often feel as though they're lacking any sort of redemptive purpose.

What's interesting about experiences of consolation and desolation is that only you know which is which. For example, I once led a team in organizing a conference. I did everything from deciding the theme to inviting the speakers to coordinating the videographer. By all accounts, the conference was excellent, and it received tremendous praise. In a way, I was very proud of what my team and I had accomplished. However, at the end of the night, I felt a heavy load in my soul. Hosting the event had pulled me away from other important obligations, and I felt that while the event was successful, I'd dropped the ball related to other priorities I had at the time. From the outside, anyone watching would have been inclined to say, "Surely that event was a consolation for Bethaney." But I knew in my soul that the event had cost me more than it had given me, landing it on my list of desolations for that season.

There are two ways you can approach the practice of examen, and I'll offer both here, starting with the way I learned. When I first began praying the examen, it was at the direction and guidance of my college campus minister during our weekly small group. She instructed us to pull out a piece of paper and draw two columns, each with three rows, for a total of six boxes. In the first column, we were instructed to write one question per row. The questions were as follows:

- When today did I feel closest to God?
- When today did I feel closest to others?
- When today did I feel closest to myself?

These were the consolations.

In the second column, we were instructed to write the following questions:

- When today did I feel farthest from God?
- When today did I feel farthest from others?
- When today did I feel farthest from myself?

These were the desolations.

We set aside ten to fifteen minutes to complete the exercise. It felt cathartic and validating to look back over my day and to see with clarity where I had experienced aliveness, connection, and joy compared to where I'd experienced heaviness, aloneness, or a sense of loss. By prayerfully tracking these consolations and desolations week after week, I started to notice patterns. I became aware of the relationships, scenarios, habits, and experiences that gave me more energy and more life. I also became aware of the activities that drained me and took more energy than they gave. This process was one of awakening to my inner life through self-reflection. Once I could see the terrain clearly, especially over many days and weeks, I had the insight needed to begin making changes.

A second way you can approach this practice is similar to the first but more free-flowing. Draw two columns, one for consolations and one for desolations. In the consolation column, write a list of any insights, experiences, or moments that energized or inspired you. In the desolation column, capture insights, experiences, and moments that drained you. Once you have your two lists, look for any patterns, reoccurring themes, or details that stick out to you.

I recommend doing this practice at least weekly, though daily is ideal for creating the habit. What you will find over time is an increased awareness of what exactly is unfolding in your inner landscape. I liken this reflection exercise to taking a daily stroll through the garden of your inner world. What is growing there? What are you proud of? What is bringing you joy? What pain is there? What relationships need tending or mending? What kind of work is filling and satisfying you? What kind of work is draining you? Mindfully walking the grounds of your inner world gives you the context you need to start making choices about the kind of life you want to lead.

All the work you've done until now has been about coming to terms with your life as it currently is and learning how to practice a more beautiful way to live. Embracing slow time, connecting with your body, and awakening to your inner terrain are the equivalent of preparing the ground of your life so you can plant new seeds of possibility. Planting is what part 2 is all about.

PAUSE & REFLECT

Over the course of part 1, you've likely done a tremendous amount of good, and challenging, work. Slowing down your life intentionally or accepting slower seasons as they come is countercultural. It takes adjustment for our minds, bodies, and souls to feel safe and at peace in this new way of moving through the world. Learning how to connect with your body, especially after periods of disregarding its voice and needs, requires patience and a willingness to wade through discomfort and any shame you might feel for having been disconnected from your body in the first place. Lastly, waking up to what's really happening in your inner life involves confrontation. If there have been emotions you've suppressed, painful situations you've avoided, or changes you've resisted making, when you slow down and finally take inventory, you'll find it's all right there. You can't run anymore. You can't hide. The only way forward is through.

If you've arrived at this point and you're sitting in what feels like a pile of discomfort and pain, I want you to know this is normal. Pain doesn't mean you're broken. Pain is there to draw your attention to what needs care. Depending on the weight of what you're carrying, I highly recommend reaching out for support. I've found that inviting others to carry the weight with me is profoundly helpful. Let a friend or counselor know about this journey you've been on. Tell them about the patterns and pain you're ready to face. Let them hold this story alongside you.

If you've arrived at this point and you're sitting in what feels like an open field full of possibility, I want you to know this is also normal. It is incredibly liberating to bravely step off the conveyor belt of hustle, urgency, and anxiety and to place your feet firmly on earthen floor. Take a deep breath. The healing you've been longing for is available. Healing doesn't mean you will never face challenging times. But you will begin to feel a sense of wholeness and safety from the inside out—even in the face of life's certain heartbreaks and difficulties. You're on your way.

Here are a few questions to deepen your reflections on the themes of part 1.

On Embracing Slow Time

1. How would you describe your current relationship to time?
2. Slow time is being present and attentive to the here and now. What helps you be more in the moment in your daily life? What keeps you from being more present in your daily life?
3. What might it look like for you to intentionally schedule slow time each week?

On Connecting with Your Body

1. What does embodiment, the experience of feeling connected and at home in your body, mean to you?
2. What in your life increases your sense of connection with your body? What in your life decreases your sense of connection with your body?

3. Complete a body scan as described in chapter 2. As you listen for your body's wisdom, what do you notice? What do you hear?

On Awakening to Your Inner Terrain

1. How would you describe your inner terrain in this season? Is it rugged and dry like the desert? Is it lush and overflowing like a rainforest? It is wild and chaotic like an unkept garden or disheveled like an abandoned junkyard? What is it like?
2. Adopting a proactive posture in life, one in which you diligently attend to what is within your realm of influence, takes tremendous practice. What helps you to focus more on what's within your influence and less on what is outside your control?
3. Complete an examen prayer. What, if anything, stands out to you? What, if anything, surprises you?

PART TWO

CULTIVATION

Four

LIVING WITH THE SEASONS

Everything had changed over the course of a few months. The life I thought I'd be living had taken a drastic turn. I had to rebuild, start over, and make meaning in this new chapter. Isn't this just so *human*? To wake up one day after a job loss, a medical emergency, a family crisis, or a move to a new place and to find yourself on the starting line of a whole new journey? We have these moments of profound uncertainty, and they call us to face an unknown future with whatever focus and tenacity we can muster.

In the midst of all the change and turmoil, my husband and I decided to build a house on an acre carved out of what used to be a patch of cattle land, buffered by a forested tree line marking the property's edge. Building a home was not in the plan, but here we were, drawing up designs, talking to contractors, negotiating construction loans, and watching as a team of highly skilled laborers brought our vision for a small black barn house to life. By now, I'd begun learning the nuances of embracing slow time and of living wide awake to the messy richness of the present moment. I'd found my way back home, back to safety, in my body through breath work and other somatic healing modalities. I'd surrendered to life's invitation for me to grow roots in rural Georgia again. With all this change and healing, a variety of questions landed at my doorstep: How do I truly build a life that is firmly established and awake to the present moment? How do I cultivate an ability to receive and accept my life as it unfolds? How can I consistently practice peacefulness, despite the turmoil in the world around me? When my inner world becomes chaotic, hurried, and anxious again, how do I make sure that living a more beautiful way is not a one-off experience but a true framework for my entire life?

The answers were to be found all around me on our humble acre of land. Nature's cycles and seasons, rhythms and songs, pulsed beneath my feet. Watching the moon flow from newness to fullness back to newness again became my most beloved way of marking time. Feeling the shift in sunlight from high noon in summer to golden hour in winter began to reset the cadence of my entire life. The contrast between the hurried and anxious ways of the world and the steady and powerful ways of the natural world was hard to miss. This land and our little black barn home became the setting where the Creator's sacred, rhythmic, and utterly majestic world began reorienting my relationship with time.

The Gift of Seasonal Living

Living with the seasons is a way of orienting our lives around the seasons of the natural world. While some points of geography know only dry and rainy seasons, in my part of the world, we experience autumn, winter, spring, and summer. We root ourselves in these natural rhythms so that as we separate from cultures of urgency, hustle, and anxiety, we have a new framework for time that replaces the old one we're leaving behind.

In part 1, we explored the practice of embracing slow time in an effort to help our bodies and souls slow down enough to grapple with the realities of our lives. In the process of slowing, we become increasingly aware of the changes we need to make—changes in our work, in our relationships, or in how we tend to our bodies and souls—to live in the moment and be well-rooted in our daily lives. As we begin the work of cultivating, there is a temptation to adopt a panicked posture even related to our own growth. This can look like obsessive introspection, wherein we feverishly track every thought, idea, or emotion. It can look like bingeing content online about healing and spiritual growth. It can even look like spending hundreds of dollars on workshops, courses, therapies, retreats, and experiences to help us feel more at home in our bodies. We can become anxious about trying to be less anxious.

I know this temptation because I've been there. As you wake up to the reality of your life, not only do you start to see possibilities with new eyes, but you also begin to confront the pain of all that isn't and hasn't been working. Pain tends to push us to urgent resolutions, even if those resolutions don't solve the problem. We'll do almost anything to make the pain stop. However, when we seek relief from our pain with the same type of urgency that drove us to become overwhelmed and afraid in the first place, we end up repeating old cycles of burnout instead of breaking through into a truly new way of life. When we're confronted with difficulties—whether of our own making or due to the simple nature of being human—we use the tools we have to get by, and there's no shame in this. If urgency and stress are the tools that have helped you navigate painful and trying times in your life, it makes sense that you'd turn to them again. The invitation, however, is to practice a new way of being with a new set of tools. Living with the seasons is one such tool. This practice gives you the means to embrace slowness, embodiment, and empowering self-reflection as regular features of your everyday experience.

There are two ways I want to invite you to think about the seasons: practically and metaphorically. Practically, living with the seasons is about paying attention to the created world and looking for through lines between your physical life and the season you're experiencing. For example, during winter, when it's cold and dark, it's typical for the human body to desire coziness, warmth, and a degree of hiddenness. In her book *Wintering: The Power of Rest and Retreat in Difficult Times*, author Katherine May says, "Plants and animals don't fight the winter; they don't pretend it's not happening and attempt to carry on living the same lives that they lived in the summer. They prepare. They adapt. They perform extraordinary acts of metamorphosis to get them through. Winter is a time of withdrawing from the world, maximizing scant resources, carrying out acts of brutal efficiency and vanishing from sight."[1] What May illustrates here is that the season of winter has felt effects on the bodies of living beings. One aspect of living with the seasons is to attend to the limits and opportunities that exist within each season. We'll explore this more in the pages to come.

The second way you're invited to consider the seasons is metaphorically. By this I mean that while you may be living through one season in the literal sense, your inner life may be experiencing a different season altogether. Winter is often marked by darkness, emptiness, and stillness. You may be experiencing an internal season of winter even though it's a bright and sunny summer day outside. You may be experiencing an internal spring, marked by hope and renewal, even as the autumn leaves fall to the ground around you. By holding the seasons both practically and metaphorically, we have two lenses through which to see the gifts of living a seasonally oriented life.

Learning About Time from the Created World

Learning from the wisdom of the created world comes more easily to some of us than to others, but I've found it to be a vital aspect of living a soul-nourishing life. We need different models and frameworks for living to help us break away from habits of anxiety and urgency and put on habits of rootedness, cooperation, and sustainable productivity. The created world—full of plants, trees, animals, storms, and change—has much to teach us about what it means to be a living creature on the earth. Nature offers insightful responses to these questions: What makes for flourishing? What makes for growth? What should we make of death? How do we honor our limits? The created world invites us to root our lives in timeless ways of being, ways that teach our bodies and souls how to slow down, how to trust, how to move with the rhythm of what's coming and going in each season. Learning about time from the created world reorients how we think about our days and expands how we experience the forward motion of the clock.

As modern people, often divorced from the cycles and seasons of nature—and from the wisdom traditions that honor earth's time—we tend to hold strongly to timelines crafted by an industrial, technological mind. We tend to think about time in terms of linear progress. We understand growth as being up and to the right, as if on a graph. In linear thinking, when we encounter a problem or challenge over and over again, we're inclined to view ourselves as failures. We say things like, "Shouldn't I be over this by now?" and we lament having to revisit the same lesson more than once. This isn't an inherently bad or harmful way of thinking; it's simply one way. The natural world invites us to consider a different way of understanding time. In the natural world, time is cyclical, not linear. In cyclical thinking, when approaching a recurring difficulty or challenge, we might say something like, "Here is another chance to deepen my understanding of this challenge. I wonder what lessons are here for me now." We can cultivate a sort of double consciousness about time, integrating a seasonal, cyclical view of time that nourishes the soul with a linear, progress-oriented view of time that drives our modern world. Each season—autumn, winter, spring, and summer—offers us rich wisdom to help make this process of integration more accessible. Living with the seasons doesn't require that you change everything about your life to form a new way of being in the world. It simply means you pay attention to and heed nature's gentle wisdom as it arrives.

The Wisdom of Each Season

As we explore the wisdom the created world offers us, I'll be describing each season as experienced in my part of the world, which is rural middle Georgia in the southeastern United States. This context matters because it's likely that, depending on where you live, your seasons are experienced differently. Take my reflections as an opportunity to reflect on your geography and the seasonal wisdom available where you are.

The Wisdom of Autumn

Our first season back on my parents' farm was autumn in late October. This was appropriate, and even poetic, as our life was experiencing a sort of death. Autumn is known for this. It is the time each year when all the growth and productivity of summer slows, even dies. The leaves go from bright green to deep reds, oranges, and yellows before turning brown and falling to the ground. All around us, we see shedding. Autumn is a time of letting go. Sometimes we experience autumn in lockstep with the calendar year—September, October, November. More often than not, however, we experience autumn-like seasons anytime life brings us an invitation to let go, to say goodbye, to welcome death in all its grief and uncertainty.

Change and loss are natural parts of life's cycle. What once flourished decays, and the losses become compost for future seasons. Whether we are saying goodbye to a place we once loved, to a role we once held, or to a relationship that has changed course, the wisdom of autumn invites us to practice shedding, releasing, and finding grace in life's endings.

Autumn is an invitation to surrender. We cannot stop change any more than we can stop the oak tree from dropping its acorns and leaves each September. Rhythms of releasing are knit into the fabric of creation, and our difficult work as humans is to make peace with the letting go. Each day is different from the next. No two years will unfold in the exact same way. We are always saying goodbye. Clinging to what was or what is makes being present nearly impossible. We have to open our hands and let go of what's leaving. Much of the stress and anxiety we experience is created by our clinging and our attachment to the status quo. Autumn not only teaches us to surrender to the changes unfolding around us and within us but also reminds us that such change is guaranteed.

Autumn is also an invitation to make room for grief. Grief is a profound and often mysterious experience. It is not always glaring or loud. Grief is like a thin, steady stream of tap water from a sink faucet. If the drain is closed off with a stopper, the steady stream of grief's waters will surely fill the sink to its brim and spill over onto the countertops and floor. This is messy and will require tending. If the sink drain is open, however, grief's waters are able to flow freely through the system. We keep the drain open by being honest about the pain we feel in the shedding. We keep the drain open by talking with loved ones and friends about how the changes we're moving through are breaking our hearts. We keep the drain open by telling the truth about our disappointments, our doubts, and our fears, by revealing the vulnerability of being in transition and in between. Grief does not disappear when we avoid it. It simply keeps flowing and overflowing in the background until we make the brave choice to unstop the drain and to let it have its way in our system. Moving through grief makes us more human, more whole. Grief is the price we pay for loving.[2]

Autumn is also an invitation to pause and revel in the earth's beauty. It is not lost on me how glorious autumntime can be. While there is much fear of and resistance to death and dying in our culture, it's as though the divine wants us to know there's also an element of otherworldly awe in such transitions. The rich golden hues of changing leaves, the smoky warmth of a bonfire on a cool night, the liminality and spiritual openness we encounter in autumn's threshold between life and death—it's all a miracle. Welcoming the wisdom of autumn enables us to truly bear witness to the magic and mystery surrounding us.

The Wisdom of Winter

In the winter, darkness descends and lingers. The ground is hard with frost, and cold stings the skin. We exhale and see our breath's warm dance in the air in front of our faces. There is a quiet and stillness. Above the surface, life grows still. The trees have shed their foliage for a time. The critters have found their caves, their burrows, and their holes for rest. Even humans slow down and embrace the coziness of blankets and fireplaces and hot pots of tea. It's a special time, maybe even my favorite time of year.

There's nothing quite like the quiet of winter. It's a contrast to the noisiness of modern life. It's as though all of creation stands at attention and waits for the conductor's instruction to breathe, dance, and play again. The stillness and silence are not to be equated with desolation. Much is alive, but this life isn't apparent above the ground. The necessary growth and sustenance of wintertime happens underground, beneath the soil, where eyes cannot see and hands cannot touch. It's a season of profound faith, as we can only hope that in the stillness, in the silence, goodness and meaning are pulsing toward renewal, vitality, and sustenance.

Taproots grow deeper in wintertime. A tree's taproot is "the primary root that grows vertically downward and gives off small lateral roots."[3] As the primary root, it is the tree's strongest and most resilient root, responsible for drawing up vital nutrients to support the rest of the tree's life system. Spiritual director and contemplative prayer practitioner Jean Lengacher says this of taproots: "The function of a taproot is to absorb water and nutrients from the soil. In addition, taproots help to provide stability by anchoring deep into the ground. Typically, taproots stabilize during the winter season when trees and plants are visibly dormant, using up residual energy and nutrients to prepare for spring."[4] This takes place under the soil, out of sight.

We, too, have taproots, or ways we experience connection to places, to others, to the earth, and even to the holy. These taproots are the immaterial ways we communicate with the world around us. Through them, we experience love, we feel known, and we give of ourselves to others. Our taproots are also the ways we receive nourishment and care from the soils we're planted in—the relationships in our lives, the communities that sustain us, and the work that gives us purpose. Whenever we experience the fulfillment that flows from being in relationship with people, places, and purposeful work, it's because we are in established connections with those aspects of the human experience. Our taproots deepen in winter and in seasons of barrenness, when they can focus on inward growth instead of outward fruitfulness. As people, we need winter seasons that provide time and space for the taproots of our inner lives to grow more deeply so that we are sustained and prepared for when springtime comes.

If we are used to living in a summertime culture, where there is productivity and abundance, it can be difficult to make peace with the silence, the stillness, and the hidden nature of winter's gifts. Winter is a time of barrenness and a lack of visible growth and productivity. When winter comes, especially by way of suffering, we tend to blame ourselves, as though we've done something wrong or haven't generated enough output. It's tempting to think we're broken in some way. The wisdom of winter, however, reminds us that for everything there is a season. Wintertime and the darkness and stillness it brings are invitations to rest, to nourish ourselves, and to be strengthened from the inside out. Without winter seasons, our roots would remain shallow.

Many years ago, a dear friend of mine shared an image online of her two home-cultivated orchid plants. If you know anything about growing orchids, you know it is a true labor of love, as they are needy, temperamental, and all-around difficult flowers to grow. The first orchid in her picture had a gorgeous and lengthy stem with bright purple-pink blossoms. It had multiple buds waiting to break open. If you'd seen this orchid in a pot at your local nursery, you would have been inclined to purchase the plant and take it home. It was stunning. But the second orchid in her image was stubby and small. The stem was about half the length of the one sitting next to it, and it didn't have any blossoms. It was the type of plant you'd overlook because, on the surface, it had very little to offer in terms of beauty and presentation.

What I found most striking in my friend's picture, however, were the roots. The roots told the truer story. While the first orchid was tall, blossoming, and beautiful, its roots were short and shallow. They were nearly translucent, as if they were starving for nutrients. The second orchid, though humble and lacking in charm, had roots three times as long, and they were bursting with green vibrancy. They were lengthy, healthy, and strong.

The tall, beautiful, blossoming orchid did not have the roots to sustain life. All its beauty was guaranteed to fade in due time. This orchid could not grow into its future because its roots were malnourished. The short, boring, unimpressive orchid had roots that would nourish its growth for a lifetime. So it is with us. We need winter and its gifts of darkness, quiet, and hiddenness that make it possible for the root systems of our lives to grow deeper, toward the nourishment and sustenance we need most.

We embrace the wisdom of winter when we allow ourselves to rest, to be cozy in our homes, and to welcome time for prayer, contemplation, and reflection. We embrace the wisdom of winter when we retreat from the busyness of the world for a time and when we look at life's barrenness not as a failure but as an opportunity to notice what's growing and evolving within the inner terrain of our lives. The wisdom of winter is that even the stillness is for our ultimate good.

The Wisdom of Spring

Spring is like waking up from a long nap to find that all you love most in the world is still breathing right there alongside you. If autumn is about grieving and letting go, and if winter is about retreat and resting, then spring is about trusting that what is meant to be will emerge in due time.

I once grew a stunning pineapple sage bush in my flower garden. During its first season in my garden, it was bursting with vibrancy during summertime but, like much else, it diminished so thoroughly in autumn and winter that I was certain our time together had come to an end. Months later, spring was upon us again, and my husband, Alex, and I were walking through the garden, taking in new growth and watering the yarrow, the mountain mints, the hydrangeas, the baptisia, the bee balms, and more. Then Alex, with delight and surprise, directed me to where the pineapple sage once stood. "Check this out, babe," he said while pointing to the ground right around his feet. Lo and behold, there was not one but eleven pineapple sage sprouts breaking forth from the earth! Apparently, the mother shrub scattered seeds of possibility, as mothers often do, even in her dying. I had the joy of watching the new generation of sages thrive.

Spring is a reminder that the truest parts of us that have lain dormant under the clay have everything they need to sprout up again in renewed form. As we begin shedding old ways of being, leaving patterns of anxiety and urgency behind, there can be a real fear that we'll lose our passion, our ambition, and our desire to make a good and fulfilling impact on the world around us. For me, I was terrified that if I slowed down, I would become boring, passionless, and irrelevant. But living through the surrender of autumn, cultivating trust in the dead of winter, and remaining openhanded and hopeful at the arrival of spring taught me that every good thing has a chance to thrive, especially after leaving behind the fear that death is the end of all things.

We experience the wisdom of spring when we open ourselves to the world after living through challenging or painful times. One of the temptations on the other side of enduring the grief of autumn or the retreat of winter is to hunker down in isolation and detachment from the world. Hunkering down can look like going out less, being less proactive in our relationships, or only going to places and trying activities we are familiar with. We can be enticed to turn inward and stay there. Spring, however, draws us out of our cozy dens and invites us to turn outward to the world again. It calls us to be open to new possibilities and to risk learning, growing, changing, and loving again.

The Wisdom of Summer

Following spring, we turn toward summer. Summer is marked by immense growth, abundance, and harvest. If you were to visit my family farm during summertime, you would be overcome by the sheer amount of produce coming up from the earth. There are melons and squashes, okra and corn. There are figs and blueberries. Tomatoes and peppers. Eggplants and cucumbers. More and more and more. The zucchini plants are especially prolific around here, and if you don't harvest the zucchini every day of summer, they are likely to grow beyond a consumable size in a mere day's time. There is so much fruitfulness in summertime that my mother fills most of her days canning and preserving, storing up summer's harvest for future seasons.

Summer's fruitfulness and productivity are not the by-products of pressure, force, and striving. The rich fruitfulness we encounter during summer seasons comes from having done the good and hard work of diligently cultivating one's life. If you've sown seeds of connection, restfulness, and ease, as nature would have it, you'll reap a harvest of connection, restfulness, and ease. If you've sown seeds of compassion and resilience, summer becomes the time when you experience a harvest of compassion and resilience. This work of cultivation is about stewarding what's growing within and aligning your outer expression with the values you hold most dear.

While I love summer's heat, playfulness, and abundance, what makes it special—at least in my part of the world—is that it doesn't last forever. Summer teaches us that seasons of harvest and fruitfulness come and go. We get to experience the joy, brightness, and levity of summer seasons when we celebrate progress toward our goals, when we see relationships restored, when we encounter healing for our bodies, and when we get to create and share our work with the world. But we also encounter the wisdom of summer when the heights of our fruitfulness and productivity begin to wane. I think of my tomato bushes at the end of summertime. Their growth slows, their branches begin to decay, and eventually they must be pulled up and placed on the compost pile as soil-building nourishment for futures seasons. Summer, like every other season, is temporary. What this means for us is that we must enjoy it while it's here, celebrate all the abundance it has to offer, and then accept that the wheel of the year will turn as autumn invites us again to let go.

Living with the Seasons to Flourish in a More Beautiful Way

Learning how to live with each season is a practical way to orient your life around a more rhythmic way of being in the world. Even if you don't experience the same four seasons as we do here in middle Georgia, you can still consider how the four seasons, as themes, are showing up in your lived experience. Here's what that might look like:

- To contemplate the wisdom of autumn, consider where in your life you're being invited to shed, to let go, and to surrender. Where are you noticing decay, and what might it look like to welcome losses instead of forcing, striving, and seeking to control reality as a means of avoiding grief?
- To contemplate the wisdom of winter, consider where in your life you're experiencing stillness, quiet, or mystery. Maybe there are big questions you're waiting to have answered, or perhaps you're longing for newness in an area that has felt empty and barren. What might it look like to honor stillness? What fears or emotions arise in you as you cultivate trust in the midst of darkness and uncertainty? How might you nourish your body and take care of your inner life as you wait?
- To contemplate the wisdom of spring, consider where in your life you're experiencing newness and possibility. Where have you been surprised or delighted by something new unfolding in your world? What

might it look like to cherish and celebrate this new beginning?

- To contemplate the wisdom of summer, consider where in your life you're being met with abundance and fruitfulness. Where has there been growth? In what ways have you been able to practice generosity due to the abundance you've been experiencing? What might it look like to celebrate and enjoy this time of harvest and productivity?

Cultivating rootedness in nature's rhythms is a practice that rewrites our inner narratives about loss, stillness, renewal, and growth. This practice anchors us in an experience of time that disrupts patterns of urgency. Living seasonally reminds the soul that there is a time for everything and a season for everything, and that we do not have to live in fear of missing out or falling behind. What is meant to grow will sprout up within our lives in due time. Nature's seasons and cycles are helpful not only as metaphors. They are tangible realities and ever-present invitations to be fully attentive and receptive to life's unfolding.

As we close this chapter, know that living with the seasons is a practice you nurture; it is not a destination for your arrival. Why? Eventually your experience of time creates a pace that is more sustainable and more life-giving than the patterns of urgency and anxiety that are so typical of modern life. Living seasonally will slow you down, will invite you to connect with your body in new ways depending on the time of year it is, and will give you additional language to describe what's happening in the inner terrain of your life. Difficult and painful seasons will come, and they will go. Beautiful and abundant seasons will come, and they will go. Learning how to embrace the seasons of life is essential to living grounded, being present, and making decisions that are aligned with who and how you want to be in the world.

Five

LISTENING FOR YOUR LONGINGS

"What do you want?"

My spiritual director's question landed in my lap like a lead weight. It was heavy and affecting. I didn't know what to do with it, much less how to respond.

What do I want? I hadn't even considered this before. The sheer notion that my desires had a seat at the table was shocking to me. I'd spent years doing what I was supposed to do and pursuing the goals others told me I should have for myself. It had never occurred to me that my longings had a role to play in my creating a settled, mindful, and peace-giving life.

I'd moved to the rural countryside but was still commuting over sixty miles each way to Atlanta for work. My spiritual direction sessions during that time were dedicated to unraveling the stories of my inner world and looking for off-ramps from the chaotic way of being I'd grown accustomed to. My work life had created more pressure than I could or wanted to handle, and rumination had become a persistent reality. On my commute to and from work, my thoughts were filled with refrains such as these:

I hate doing this.
I want to quit my job.
I want to move to a new city.
I don't want to do this anymore.
Maybe if I screw up enough, they'll fire me.
I just need a nap.
I need someone to save me.

Even though I was doing work I thought would make me happy, burnout was knocking at my door. While I didn't know the specifics of how I'd find my way through such a taxing situation, one thing I *did* know was that I longed for a different experience of how I was living my life.

Longings Are a Compass

While "more beautifully" is a way for all of us to live, the particularities as to how you do so are as unique as you are. What makes for a good and soul-nourishing life for one person is completely different from what makes for goodness and soul-nourishment in another person's life. One way to begin giving definition to what this new way of living means for you specifically is to listen for your longings. Your longings are a compass. They hold insight into what you value and what your dreams are. They point toward what you believe is most worth your time, talent, treasure, and energy. Longings are powerful in their ability to give direction and meaning to life.

Listening for your longings is an essential practice as you pave a new way of being. One of the first losses you endure when you're moving quickly and living reactively is your ability to access the deeper longings of your soul. You don't have margin to listen deeply, to ask big questions, or to see if and how your daily choices are aimed toward a grander vision. By embracing slow time, connecting with your body, awakening to your inner terrain, and living with the seasons, you can create the conditions necessary to determine what you truly desire. You can step off the hamster wheel that is running your life, pause long enough to become oriented to reality, and then start answering the question "Where do I go from here?"

How Pain Points Us Toward Our Longings

At first, I didn't know I was longing for slowness or for the gifts it might offer me. Many years prior to this period of commuting back and forth from my parents' farm to the city, I had worked in nonprofit urban agriculture. After a few years of managing urban farms in Atlanta, I accepted a job designing programs for social entrepreneurs. The shift was palpable. My work changed from managing farm operations to being led by a supervisor, and from days outdoors in the garden to days inside at a desk. My work shifted from growing food to growing ideas. It was a big change, and a welcomed one.

What I love about transitions is that they instigate opportunities for us to pause and evaluate how we are approaching life. They create an opportunity for us to ask ourselves how we want to show up differently in the world. We get to reflect on the person we've been while setting expectations for the kind of person we want to be. Transitions are often times of possibility and creativity, which on the one hand is exciting and on the other hand is unnerving as our sense of purpose and identity is shaken up by the changes we're enduring. It can feel as if the ground beneath our feet is beginning to shake and break open. All bets are off.

My new work felt grand, and the stakes seemed high. While I'd loved the daily, steady work of tending to the one-acre urban farm in the middle of the city, it wasn't the most publicly visible work. This new job, however, felt incredibly visible. With each event, retreat, and conference we held, I felt the pressure to perform intensify. My work ethic matched the degree of pressure I felt, compelling me to arrive early and work late when I could. I took voracious notes at every learning opportunity and asked lots of questions, absorbing as much insight as I could about how to do my work well. Over time, my mantra became "Just add value," and I extended myself to over-deliver on each task. The achievement and the applause were fuel, and they sustained me for a time.

Eventually, however, I began noticing a persistent sort of anxiety, a clenching tightness in my chest. I could often breathe through it, at least until it refracted into blends of anger, impatience, and frustration. Perhaps you've known this anxiety too. It can feel like an annoying buzz in the corner of your mind, constant and unyielding. It can manifest as irritation in its earliest forms or as an inability to focus or listen well. It's especially disrupting when you desperately want to be present to those around you, but the quality of presence you hope for feels just out of reach. It's an uncomfortable sort of energy, one that leaves you fidgety, restless, and maybe even quick-tempered. It's the hum of agitation and the sense that nothing is or ever will be good enough.

I used to believe that our longings, those yearned-for desires within us, would emerge from only the positive, mountaintop experiences we have, such as when we dream bigger for our lives while we're on vacation or how inspiration strikes when we experience great food, great sex, or great art. I think of the ways our spirits lift when a loved one returns our affection for them and the ways we hope for such a connection to last for a lifetime. These sorts of hopeful, beautiful, joy-filled longings—both yearned for and fulfilled—are what used to come to mind for me when I considered answering the questions "What are your desires?" and "What do you want?" My heart and mind would fill with rainbows, butterflies, and all sorts of happy pictures of what could be possible.

This way of identifying longings, however, turned on its head when I found myself on edge, irritable, and frustrated every single day. I was confused and disoriented by how difficult it was to enjoy the very responsibilities I wanted. It was in this unexpected experience that I learned a key lesson about how longings actually show up in our stories. Yes, maybe we do tap into something of our deepest yearnings when we're on life's mountaintops, but more often than not, the truest longings of our souls are made evident in the toughest valleys we sojourn through. It is easy to see hopeful possibilities from the perspective of life's highlight reels, but our true desires and deepest yearnings—those seeds—break through only in the dark. The difficult parts of our stories hold the nuggets of wisdom we need to discover a new way to live.

Practically speaking, one of the keys to unlocking the longings I carried was to listen closely to my inner chatter and to inquire about the true longing underlying each recurring refrain. My inner chatter, in this instance, was characterized by urgency, anxiety, and fear. My inner inquirer was characterized by curiosity and a desire to find the deeper truth beneath the angst. Here is a snippet of how this inner dialogue unfolded:

Inner chatter: I hate doing this.

Inner inquirer: I believe you. Why do you think that is?

Inner chatter: I'm not sure. I'm just so tired all the time.

Inner inquirer: Yes, maybe you actually hate this, or maybe you're longing for rest.

Here is another example:

Inner chatter: I want to quit my job.

Inner inquirer: What is it about your job that makes you want to quit?

Inner chatter: My supervisor keeps adding more to my plate even though I've communicated that I am at capacity and can't take on more work right now.

Inner inquirer: You can quit your job, but it also sounds as though you're longing for your boundaries to be respected.

In both of these instances, the prevalent thought or challenge held within it a seed of a deeper longing. I longed for rest. I longed for my boundaries to be respected. I could quit my job, and eventually I did, but identifying my longings was essential because what I longed for was a compass pointing me toward the new life I wanted to create.

Here are versions depicting the longings buried within my fears and frustrations:

I hate doing this.

You're longing for a space to breathe and consider your options.

I want to quit my job.

You're longing for your limits to be honored and for respectful treatment.

I want to move to a new city.

You're longing for inspiration, a change of scenery.

I don't want to do this anymore.

You're longing for a break and some space to breathe.

Maybe if I screw up enough, they'll fire me.

You're longing for support and ease in your decision-making.

I just need a nap.

You're longing for a break and some undisturbed sleep.

I need someone to save me.

You're longing for help and protection.

Beneath the surface of the recurring, painful thoughts filling my mind day-in and day-out were tiny directives inviting me to rearrange my life. I didn't understand this while in the middle of it all; I thought I was just frustrated with my work and sad because I felt stuck in a stressful situation. What I've learned, however, is that even the most challenging seasons we live through offer us gifts of insight about the healing we need most. When we approach our dissatisfaction, our frustration, and even our sadness with curiosity, they have a world of wisdom to offer us about the kind of life we actually want to be leading. The negative emotions we feel are check engine lights of our inner lives pointing us toward the care, attention, and restoration we need.

This lesson hit home when I found myself sitting across the table from my husband, unpacking what it would look like for us to enter a new season of our marriage. We were in the thick of discussing a wide array of relational dynamics, evolving faith practices, emotional needs, and more. As we talked and listened to each other share from our distinct experiences, I felt a sadness rise in my chest like a sudden storm, like waves churning on my insides, ready to burst forth in streams of tears.

We hadn't addressed it directly yet, but moving from the city to rural cattle country, even though the right decision at the time, was a costly choice. While I needed a break from the hustle and bustle of city life, and while embracing the slower pace of this new setting had worked wonders for my health and overall well-being, a quiet longing had been growing large and loud in the recesses of my heart. I'd been putting a lot of pressure on my husband to meet all my emotional and relational needs. It was more than should be asked of one person. While he was doing his very best, he couldn't fill the relational holes that had been created by our relocation, and I hadn't yet done the work to build a new community of friends in this new place. In this moment of conversation across the dinner table, I came face-to-face with a pain I'd been carrying ever since we moved: I was deeply lonely, and I'd been feeling isolated and unknown. While I'd turned to my normal coping mechanism of overworking and trying to control every variable of my life to compensate for the loneliness I'd been feeling, in my conversation with my husband, I acknowledged the longing for community that was bursting from the soil of my life. This breaking open was painful, as confronting the truth often is. But it was also what I needed to start making different choices about how I was investing in friendships in my life.

My longing for friendship was found in the process of honoring the pain of my loneliness. If you are struggling to know what your longings are, if you can't quite put your finger on the deeper needs within, look to the painful places. Look to the places of heartbreak, frustration, and disappointment. You will surely find the seeds of your longings there.

This practice of identifying our longings by way of attending to challenging or seemingly negative experiences is beneficial not just for us as individuals. When we endeavor to live a more beautiful way, we can identify the longings we have for our world, for our neighbors, and for our communities by attending to the issues that fill us with anger or even outrage. The topics or situations that spark ferocity in us, especially socially or politically, point us toward our longings for the world. If you are angry about unjust wars or the demise of the most marginalized, then you long for pathways of justice and peacemaking. If you are angry about the lack of diverse representation in communities of faith, then perhaps you long for faith traditions to truly serve and care for all people. If you are angry about the deep disconnection across lines of political difference, then perhaps you long for a shared sense of identity and care that transcends political divides. When identifying our longings, it's important that we consider not just the longings we have for our individual lives but also the longings we have for the world we're cocreating alongside one another.

The Wild Mother is a creative floral design studio based in Oklahoma City that uses the stunning nature of florals to cultivate a collective imagination for healing and social justice. Led by a team of three Afro-Indigenous, Afro-Latina sisters named Lauren, Leah, and Callie Palmer, the studio combines the beauty of flowers and the power of storytelling to amplify the lived experiences and felt needs of historically marginalized and presently brutalized communities in their region. One of the Wild Mother's mottos is "art is medicine."[1] This simple phrase, attributed to Leah, speaks to the ways in which creativity, artistry, craft, and color all converge to help us heal from racial trauma, gender-based violence, the harmful impacts of settler colonialism, and more.

On the hundredth anniversary of the race massacre in the Greenwood District of Tulsa—a tragedy in which mobs of white residents attacked and destroyed the lives, businesses, and homes of Black residents in the city—the three sisters, having listened to the pain and needs of their community, invited the public to commemorate and grieve through a campaign called "Send Flowers To." Sending flowers is a cultural practice for both celebrating joyous moments and grieving profound losses. Through this campaign, community members were invited to send flowers to Greenwood, where The Wild Mother then created a floral installation that allowed the community to lament and to remember what had transpired there one hundred years prior. The sisters' responsiveness and creativity fulfilled in a profound and lasting way their city's deep longing to honor and commemorate those who'd been harmed by racial violence.

How Our Inner Terrain Helps Us Identify Our Longings

In addition to approaching the pain points in your life with curiosity, you can also discover your longings by paying close attention to what is unfolding within your inner terrain. Take note of what sparks joy, creativity, and possibility within you. Take note of what drains you and leaves you feeling empty. One way to capture this information on a regular basis is through the prayer of examen we discussed in part 1 of this book. By reflecting on the consolations and desolations in your daily life, you can find not only patterns pointing to the deeper longings you carry but also practical direction for bringing those longings to life.

As a spiritual director, I've had the privilege of working with many individuals who through intentional reflection have come to know what they're longing for and have made decisions to bring those longings to life. One of my favorite examples is a young woman who lived in Austin, Texas. She loved living in Austin and envisioned that she'd be there for the rest of her life. However, through a series of painful losses, she ended up having to move away from her beloved city and in with family, many states away, for a time. When she and I began meeting, she was navigating a spiritual, emotional, and relational wilderness. She felt low, sad, disconnected, and alone. As a spiritual director, I knew it wasn't my job to make her pain go away, as if I could. It was my job to listen, to bear witness, to notice how she and the divine were working together to help her find her way. Over the course of our monthly meetings, she continued to return to the question of whether she should move back to Austin. Month after month we processed what the city meant to her, how she'd grown and changed while there, and what possibilities might be available to her if she returned. Watching her talk about moving back was inspiring, as I could see the joy on her face and the lightness in her spirit. Something was calling her back; her longing was speaking to her. Then one day she shared the great news: She'd found a job in Austin and had plans to move within a few weeks. She'd looked for lodging and a church, and in her own words, "All the doors just kept opening." She moved and started a new life, abiding in her values for faith and community, aware of both the pain and the joy held in her memory of this city she loved, and fully receptive to whatever this leg of her adventure would hold. She was able to identify this longing because rather than feeling resigned to the circumstances at her door, she looked at her life and paid attention to the stirrings and needs of her soul. Then she made a decision that aligned with her ultimate vision. She and I continued to meet online for a few months after her move, and life continued on with its ups and downs. She dated and had breakups, she had to change apartments due to an issue with the building, and she had health challenges to work through. Life kept happening. But she'd listened to her longing and heeded its wisdom, so even though hard things still happened, she was able to meet them with the fullness of her presence and commitment.

This is the power of identifying your longings. Doing so will help you meet the deepest needs of your heart so that you can live awake to your life. What do you want? And what will it take for you to go after it?

Two Things We Need When Listening for Our Longings

As you go about listening for your longings, both by way of the pain points in your life and by noticing the activity happening in your inner terrain, there are two things you need: patience and vulnerability.

Patience

Longings are like seeds. They hold tremendous potential as they wait to sprout, take root, and bear fruit. They are not always apparent on the surface; you may not even know they are there. This is why embracing slow time, connecting to your body, and awakening to your inner terrain are such important parts of the process. When you slow down, connect, and reflect—on both what brings you joy and what breaks your heart—you will bump into those seeds of desire as they ask for a little room to grow.

For some, accessing the true desires of their hearts is easy. They know what they want, and they're prepared to make changes to fulfill their longings. For others, the process of naming and taking ownership of their desires is more challenging. If you grew up in a setting where your needs and wants were dismissed or invalidated, it can take time to recover a sense that your desires matter at all. If your personality is bent toward pleasing and serving others, then you may struggle to know what you want and to believe your desires are worth pursuing. You may need more time to give voice to what your longings are. You may not have answers right away. You may need to spend weeks praying the examen or exploring your inner terrain. I want to encourage you to take your time. Be patient and gracious with yourself and with your unique timeline. There is no rush. If you feel the temptation to push for answers before you're ready, return to the foundational practices laid out in part 1: Embrace slow time, connect with your body, and awaken to your inner terrain. Once you've experienced a degree of renewal through these practices, return to the invitations of this chapter: Practice curiosity about your pain points and reflect on your consolations and desolations through the prayer of examen. And when possible, invite a counselor, spiritual director, or trusted companion to walk alongside you in this process.

Vulnerability

Our longings are not always quick to reveal their true nature, and it can feel risky to give voice to exactly what we need. There is often the fear that if we're honest, our longings will be disregarded or our needs will go unmet. So rather than doing the vulnerable work of listening for and naming our longings, then making the necessary adjustments to live in alignment with our longings, we busy ourselves with distraction or with managing pain instead of resolving root issues. For example, I felt vulnerable admitting to myself, "I need to have a hard conversation with my boss about my boundaries." I felt vulnerable sitting across the table from my husband and saying, "I'm so sorry for putting so much pressure on you. I'm lonely and I'm afraid I don't have what it takes to build community here." We feel vulnerable showing up and advocating for our social values when we know an institution, political or religious, may go on to make decisions that we recognize as harmful. There is an inherent vulnerability to the seed-like state of our longings that inclines us to disregard or hide them. However, a more beautiful way unfolds when we confront uncomfortable emotions and we let our longings show us what they truly are.

If you feel vulnerable or uncomfortable being honest about what you're longing for, know that this is normal. You feel vulnerable because your desires are valuable. As you begin to name your longings, resist the temptation to edit yourself. Resist the temptation to judge or critique your inner voice. Resist the temptation to give voice to only the longings that seem "realistic." Let yourself dream. Be honest, even as you feel all the vulnerability and riskiness of finally articulating what you really want.

In what follows, we'll dig into the work of discerning which longings should be nurtured and which are best left in the world of dreaming. Before we get there, I'd like you to pause for a moment to notice whatever is stirring within you as you consider this task of listening for your longings and using them as a compass to find your unique expression of living in a well-rooted, life-giving way. My longings included living in a slower place and having more flexible work. I came to know these longings by paying attention to my pain and processing with my spiritual director how my working life was impacting my time, body, and soul. Your longings will look different depending on your roles, your personality, the season of life you're in, and more. Here are a few questions to help you begin naming your specific longings. Grab a journal or a piece of paper in order to respond.

- What pain points are most evident in your life right now? What longings might they be pointing to?
- Whom can you invite to process these pain points with you?
- Look back over the past week. What moments or experiences brought you joy? What moments or experiences drained you? Given these reflections, what might you be longing for?
- What needs to change in order for you to lead a more tethered, centered life?

Discerning Which Longings to Nurture

The first house my husband Alex and I lived in after getting married was a small duplex in a suburb just outside Atlanta. In many ways, the house was a perfect starter home. It was brick with hardwood floors. There were two tiny bedrooms separated by a bathroom so small you could barely stand up in front of the toilet without bumping the edge of the sink positioned on the opposing wall. The home was cozy and warm, and it was ours.

Alex and I met while working together at an organic garden nursery, raising and selling herbs, vegetables, and perennial shrubs for our local community. We designed and installed edible foodscapes for elementary schools and local families. We talked to neighbors about their gardening hopes and recommended the best plants for their specific yards. We also helped people navigate their gardening concerns by proposing natural solutions to the many challenges that can plague a small garden. We loved growing things and helping others find their way in the gardening world. With this passion in heart and mind, we both had a heartfelt desire, a longing, to plant a garden at our starter home.

I was committed to the task. I wanted to build a small greenhouse-like frame and fill it with tiny seedlings that could be transplanted behind our home. Alex, in his wisdom, had doubts. "The backyard is much too shaded," he said. "Babe, this is a great idea, but there's not enough sun exposure here to grow what you have in mind."

I was persistent, and he was patient. He was also right. The house was nearly perfect, but there wasn't enough sun exposure in the backyard. The seeds I set out to grow didn't make it from their growing trays into the pots situated in the brightest spot we could find.

I was disappointed. I had a vision in my mind about what the fullest expression of my longing would look like, and I was sad to discover that my vision wouldn't come to life. This disappointment, however, had a seed of wisdom within it: Growth is conditional. I learned that you can do your best to name your longings and to set them up for success, but you can't control the world and you must work within the constraints of life itself.

Identifying your longings through curiosity about the areas of pain in your life and by paying careful attention to the inner terrain of your life is just the beginning. The work that follows is discerning which longings are worth your yes and whether the conditions of your life can actually accommodate their growth. Planting a small garden for our starter home was worth our yes, but the conditions—the placement of our house, the shade created by the already growing shrubbery and trees in the yard—made my longing to grow the garden I desired impossible. So it is with our lives and the deep yearnings of our hearts. We must listen for what our longings are, but once we name them, we must ask, "Can this grow *here*? Can this grow *now*?" This is the work of discernment.

Discernment is the practice of listening for direction, insight, and guidance. It is a practice of decision-making with etymological roots that speak to the work of "separating" and "dividing, by sifting."[2] Consider holding all your longings like seeds in your hand. The process of discernment involves sifting through all you're holding and separating what is to be planted from what is to be discarded or composted. In the Christian tradition, discernment is not only about this practical work of sifting and separation but also about making difficult choices between God's best for you and anything that would diminish your ability to live toward that vision. In her book *The Way of Discernment*, Elizabeth Liebert says, "Discernment . . . is the process of intentionally becoming aware of how God is present, active, and calling us as individuals and communities so that we can respond with increasingly greater faithfulness."[3] What I appreciate about this definition is how it reminds us that discerning which longings to plant, nurture, and cultivate is not merely a choice we make based on a whim or out of convenience. Discerning which longings to nurture is a spiritual process through which we engage our deepest selves and the divine. Not all longings emerge at the right place and right time. Not all longings are beneficial, valuable, or even true. Not all longings serve the highest good of ourselves and others.

This is why discernment—a process of sifting and sorting, of discriminating between options—matters.

Our hearts are full of passion and possibility. Whether due to nature or nurture, whether ascribed to original glory or original sin, our hearts have the capacity to guide us to both beautiful and destructive places. Ancient wisdom traditions speak of the heart's wickedness and deceitfulness, illuminating a fundamental heart sickness that is part and parcel of human nature (Jer. 17:9). Ancient wisdom traditions also speak of the heart's instruction (Ps. 16:7), of its potential for wisdom (90:12), and of its ability to be the wellspring of life (Prov. 4:23). As we approach the work of discernment, we must remember that we are not all good or all evil, nor are we all light or all shadow. We have capacity for both. When it comes to discerning whether or how to nurture a specific longing in our lives, we must first acknowledge our inclinations toward selfish gain, self-protection, and self-aggrandizing and the many ways we make much of our own wants to the detriment of our neighbors. If we are unable to rightly assess our ability to create chaos and cause harm, we will be poor stewards of our ability to cultivate beauty and create healing in the world. Acknowledging the very real possibility of harm and chaos flowing from our lives is not meant to lessen our self-esteem or make us feel small. Quite the opposite. When we can tell the truth, in humility, about how flawed we really are, we are empowered to pursue the good and virtuous from a place of self-awareness.

A friend and I were once discussing the role of emotional intelligence in leadership. She and I were both in the daily grind of building new organizations, and we were unpacking the responsibility we felt to be good stewards of our own emotional worlds. Leadership in any capacity requires that you be highly attuned to your own patterns of impact, because, as a leader, your choices have the ability to create chaos or to create connection for the people following you. During our conversation, my friend expressed that her daughter, at the tender age of four years old, was demonstrating incredible emotional intelligence. "She has such high EQ. It's like she always knows how to read the room," she said. "And she's so *manipulative*." We both burst into laughter at the truth of this. Manipulation is the ability to read a situation and influence the variables to your own advantage, which is a shadow side of emotional intelligence. Emotional intelligence is the ability to leverage one's skill of perception to influence variables to the advantage of others. Every bright light casts a shadow. The shadow becomes dangerous, harmful, or destructive when we refuse to acknowledge its existence and its power. I imagine that my friend's awareness of her daughter's emotional intelligence will help her teach her how to steward her perceptive abilities with thoughtfulness and care.

Our longings function in a similar way. They also have shadow sides. This is why discernment is critical. A longing for slowness can have a shadow side of self-centeredness. A longing for connection can have a shadow side of codependency. A longing for justice in the world can have a shadow side of control and hatred of the other. Discerning our longings, holding the seeds of our desires with wisdom and maturity, means telling the truth about the nuanced dynamics unfolding within our souls. Much of the social fracturing, political turmoil, and violence we witness on the world stage flows from disordered wanting. As we aim to embody a more beautiful way in the world, we must be honest about our own disordered longings so that we can make decisions that are not only for our personal good but also for the good of our neighbors, our communities, and the world around us. I don't mean to deter you from exploring your longings as they are. But we must use thoughtful reflection so that we don't create chaos and harm in our efforts to meet our own needs.

Slowing down to listen to my pain was the first step to determining my longings. I was able to identify my longing for rest and my longing for boundaries. I didn't know it at the time, but discernment—prayerfully and thoughtfully sorting and sifting to determine *how* to approach fulfilling those longings—would have been an ideal step number two. I, however, was not the most practiced at discernment in that season. Upon realizing that I needed rest and boundaries, instead of discerning how to approach getting those needs met, I just quit my job. I put in my notice, I watched one of my biggest projects fall into a tailspin, I burned some relational bridges, and I justified my choice because that was easier than confronting how I'd let fearfulness and anxiety make the decision for me. Many years on the other side of that experience, I wonder how the story could have unfolded differently if I'd had the wisdom, patience, and self-knowing to prayerfully discern how to fulfill the longings I had. What boundaries could I have set? What relationships could I have protected? What creative arrangements could I have made? Discernment slows us down and helps us make decisions from a conscious place within ourselves.

For years I felt embarrassed about the haste of my decision to quit my job, but time and self-compassion have taught me that life is full of lessons like these and that it's okay to make mistakes. If you notice that urgency, fear, and anxiety have compelled you to make decisions you otherwise would not have made, know that you are not alone. We are all unlearning here. The reality is that even if I'd followed the discernment process to a tee, there are still no guarantees life would have unfolded easily and without any complications. Discernment does not guarantee positive outcomes. Discernment can, however, create conditions for the good seeds of our longings to take root and grow into life-giving possibilities.

Discernment requires a process of reflection. Below is a reflection exercise you can use to discern whether a specific longing is one you'd like to give your yes to. Grab your journal or a piece of paper to use as you work through the prompts that follow.

Bring to mind a longing you've felt emerging from beneath the surface of your life. This may be one you wrote down earlier or one that has come to mind more recently. If your longing came to mind quickly, hold it close. If you're unsure of what this longing might be, remember that pain often contains seeds of longings. Pause and listen to your body. Do you feel a tightness in your chest or a fluttering in your gut? Maybe a knot in your throat or a pulsing sensation in your lower back? Slow down. Listen. Sit with your observations.

What are you longing for? Rest, connection, reconciliation, ease? Joy, playfulness, peace of mind, sobriety? Take note.

As you're holding this longing in your heart and mind, turning it over in your spirit, contemplate the following questions:

- In what ways is this longing opening you to a deeper connection with yourself?
- In what ways is this longing opening you to richer connections with others?
- In what ways is this longing inviting you into deeper communion with the sacred, the holy, and the good?

Take note of any thoughts, images, directions, or insights that come to mind. These are related to consolation, connection, and prospective joy.

When you're ready, transition to the next set of questions:

- In what ways is this longing closing you off from a deeper connection with yourself?
- In what ways is this longing closing you off from richer connections with others?
- In what ways is this longing drawing you out of communion with the sacred, the holy, and the good?

Take note of any thoughts, images, directions, or insights that come to mind. These are related to desolation, disconnection, and prospective sadness or despair.

As you're holding this particular longing in heart and mind, consider that the longings that draw you into deeper connection with yourself, others, and the holy are perhaps the ones for which you may want to make more room. Also consider that the longings that draw you into disconnection from yourself, others, and the holy are the ones you may want to lay on the compost pile to be transformed into nourishment for another time. Remember, our lives hold both light and shadow. This is nothing to be ashamed or afraid of. It's information we get to use as we decide what to do with the longings of our hearts.

Ultimately, the invitation here is to take note and make observations. So much of living a more beautiful way is about becoming more aware, and the practical application of that is unique to you. The aim is to tip the scale toward rest and contemplation so that your actions are sustainable and fortifying to both yourself and those around you. Clarity may not come quickly, but I've found it nearly always comes with time.

What a More Beautiful Way Means to You

This part of the journey, of listening for your longings and making choices to make them a reality, can be a critical turning point for your story. This is where you say no to habits of urgency and anxiety and yes to rhythms, activities, places, and priorities that mean the most to you, where you align your energy with the deepest values of your heart. Your longings are the compass pointing toward your expression of a soul-satisfying, sustainably paced life in which you are able to welcome your days as they come and stand firm in the face of life's challenges. The details of how this way comes to life vary depending on your unique context. Who are you? Where do you live? What relationships are most important to you? What kind of work inspires and delights you? What pain are you carrying? What hardships are at your door? All these details and more give shape to what living a more beautiful way means for you. As you practice cultivation, you'll build the soul-strength to welcome all of life as it comes.

Six

MAKING ROOM FOR NEW GROWTH

I walked along the garden trail with pruners in hand. The head gardener of our nursery had given me instructions: "Deadhead the rose bushes." To "deadhead" the rose bushes meant to clip off all the roses that at one time had been stunning and vibrant but had since shriveled up to their natural end. Removing the decayed and dying rose blossoms was a practice of making room for the healthy and still blooming flowers to thrive.

The head gardener came outside and surveyed my work. "Good job," he said. "Now we have to prune some of the open blossoms too."

I was caught off guard. Why on earth would we cut back perfectly healthy, beautiful rose blossoms? Wasn't this the point of the rose bush, to be stunning and full of bright and tender growth? I didn't understand. I watched our head gardener walk alongside the shrubs and clip bright pink blossoms. They fell to the ground, and I collected them as I was able. He explained to me as he moved along, "You see all these rose buds that haven't opened yet? We have to remove not only the dead blossoms but also some of the open ones in order to make room for these new buds to blossom in their time. We're concerned about not just the individual rose blossoms but the health and life cycle of the entire shrub. We prune because we want to see this rose bush create as many flowers as possible over the course of the season. It's counterintuitive, but it's the way these things work."

I immediately resonated with the wisdom embodied in this pruning practice. Several phrases from the head gardener's explanation echoed in my spirit:

> ". . . new buds to blossom in their time."
>
> ". . . the health and life cycle of the entire shrub."
>
> "It's counterintuitive, but it's the way these things work."

His comments drew up from within me a remembrance of Jesus's words in the Christian Scriptures: "I am the true vine, and my Father is the gardener. He cuts off every branch in me that bears no fruit, while every branch that does bear fruit he prunes so that it will be even more fruitful" (John 15:1–2 NIV).

Cutting back, saying goodbye, releasing what was, embracing rejection and loss and change—these are all ways the practice of pruning moves in and through our lives, facilitating new growth and possibilities. To embrace pruning, caused by both the hand of divine love and our own choices, is to embrace the dynamic nature of life itself. When we are in the throes of shedding and letting go, the pain of the experience might incline us to think that something harmful or destructive is underway. To understand the practice of pruning, however, is to know that even our greatest losses and moments of surrender are actually creating the exact conditions necessary for our being to grow into its fullest expression.

Pruning not only invites us to shed the decaying and dying limbs of our lives but also invites us to determine what good things must be shed in order to make room for the greater possibilities longing to be birthed in our lives and stories.

The Purpose of Pruning

To prune means to cut back, to trim, and to remove. It is the act of taking shears to the limbs of what's growing and cutting off what no longer facilitates healthy growth. A good gardener will tuck her pruning shears into her belt harness nearly each day so that she can quickly and efficiently cut back whatever is hindering progress as she moves through the winding paths of all she's cultivating that season. I think of trimming the suckers off tomato plants or cutting back the basil flowers to extend the growing season of the herb. I think of plucking the early strawberries to encourage further root growth. In all these cases, the gardener prunes to make sure that the plant's resources are directed toward the most important priority: fruitfulness.

The same holds true for our lives, in terms of both how we utilize our time and how we manage our thoughts, beliefs, emotions, and all sorts of habits of heart and mind. Cutting back in terms of our time involves looking at what sorts of activities are filling our days and assessing to what extent those activities are moving us toward fruitfulness. In regard to our inner lives, we take inventory of the thought patterns, beliefs, emotions, and more to determine how they are shaping our flourishing. It is worth noting that fruitfulness and flourishing are not synonymous with ease; in fact, growth, even of the good and right things in our lives, is often uncomfortable and costly. To prune is to do our very best to point the life-giving energy of our lives toward the most meaningful, though perhaps challenging, work that our lives are inviting us to do. Pruning is not for the sake of cutting alone. We prune to create conditions for whole, living beings to thrive. The act of pruning always has its eye toward wholeness, toward vibrancy, toward the highest good of whatever living system is being transformed.

Have you ever seen what happens in a small patch of forest when larger trees or shrubs are cut back and removed? Sunlight is able to reach the forest floor in ways it couldn't before, and new vegetation, in receiving the sun's rays, is able to grow. It is profound to witness what unfolds as sunlight touches previously inaccessible places. Pruning welcomes warmth and renewal, which allows the seeds their chance to break forth from the forest floor, generating new life.

As we prune our schedules, to-do lists, and ways we spend our time, and as we prune those habits of heart and mind whose seasons have come to an end, we are redirecting the energy of our lives toward fruitfulness. We are making room for new growth in the nooks and crannies of our stories. This work is equal parts practical and mystical, a felt human reality and an otherworldly one. To prune and make room for new life is to cocreate with the divine.

The Process of Pruning

It rarely snows in middle Georgia, and yet there we were on a cold January morning watching closely as snowflakes fell from the sky and gently covered the ground. It was beautiful, and I was grateful to be there as a witness to the wonder of it all.

My brother had invited my husband Alex and me over to his house to help him assess how to best prune the peach and pear trees in his backyard. "It's best to prune the trees in the winter months," Alex said. I asked him to elaborate. "Well, the sap isn't running during the cold months, and the life energy of the tree is in the root zone, so when you cut back a branch, you're not causing a shock to the system like you would if you tried to prune during the height of summer. It's the difference between cutting off your fingernail and cutting off your finger. You're trying to prevent shock. During the winter months, the trees are in a state of dormancy; they're kind of asleep, so when you prune them, it causes less harm."

We got bundled up and made our way outside. Before cutting anything, Alex stood back and observed the peach tree for some time. I suppose he was contemplating the structure of the tree itself, taking in its growth patterns, making mental notes about how the tree might want to bear fruit in the coming season. I imagine that while examining the tree he was asking himself questions: Which of these branches stands the best chance of bearing good fruit? Which are core to this tree's strength? and Which are getting in the way, hindering the tree's health and potential?

Eventually, Alex hopped up into the branches with his pruning shears in hand. He promptly got to work cutting back the branches whose time had come. There was a method to his process. He occasionally articulated why he'd selected some branches and not others. In some cases, he removed a branch because it was scarred and damaged in a way that couldn't be restored. Leaving it on the tree would direct the tree's life force toward trying to heal that branch instead of toward bearing fruit, so the branch had to be pruned. There were cases in which a branch was preventing stronger, hardier branches from receiving sunlight, so he pruned it in order to create pockets of openness in the tree's frame. There were also scenarios in which Alex cut off some of the smaller branches growing out from larger branches so that the larger branches had fewer branches to sustain. Cutting back smaller branches meant that when the tree was full of fruit, the larger branches would be able to withstand the weight without snapping. A snapped branch, full of fruit in the height of summer, would compromise the entire tree.

When to Prune

I learned numerous lessons about the nature of life and the necessity of cutting back while watching my husband prune the peach and pear trees on that cold winter morning. The first lesson was about when to prune. How do we know when it's the right time to step back, evaluate, and make the decision to let something go? Inasmuch as our lives are like trees, it's best not to prune and cut back on commitments, transition out of relationships, or push for drastic change at the height of activity, chaos, or busyness. When we're in seasons of busyness, perhaps feeling overextended and overwhelmed, it can be challenging to see life clearly. It's like driving ninety miles an hour, with our days and weeks passing in a blurry haze. These busy seasons of our lives that are bursting with activity tend to force us to focus our energy on surviving and bearing fruit. Pruning, quitting, or cutting things off while in the midst of such pressure and activity can lead to rushed decisions. While rushed decisions are necessary from time to time, better decisions tend to come when we have time to step back, observe the ins and outs of our lives, and make decisions from a place of thoughtfulness.

Watching my husband prune the fruit trees in winter underscored for me the importance of allowing life to calm down enough so we can see clearly and assess rightly what needs pruning and resist the temptation to prune in the midst of overwhelm. If you are sensing the need to shed some aspect of your life, look for or create a moment to pause and reflect. Even a small window of time will do. Let yourself slow down enough for your inner world to grow quiet and calm. You don't have to go on a lengthy retreat to create this moment of pause for yourself. See if you can carve out an intentional ten or twenty minutes to sit still, be quiet, and let the dust of your life settle so that you can approach your pruning work with a calm spirit, an open heart, and a clear mind.

What to Prune

Another lesson I learned watching Alex prune the fruit trees was about what to prune, and at least three criteria seemed to be top of mind for him: (1) the damage sustained by certain branches, (2) the extent to which a branch was a distraction, preventing the sunlight from penetrating into the tree's growth system, and (3) the various branches' capacity and whether they could realistically hold the weight of fruit all season.

When determining what to prune from our lives, we can use a similar matrix: (1) What in my life is damaged in such a way that a tremendous amount of energy and resources is being consumed to repair it and keep it alive? (2) What is distracting me from the deeper fruitfulness and growth I'm longing for? (3) What can I realistically hold? Where do I need to prune, even within the areas of my life where I've traditionally experienced fruitfulness, so that even more fruit will grow in due season?

Pruning What's Been Damaged

I am notoriously hopeful and tend to believe that almost every broken thing can be fixed, healed, or mended in due time. I am not the best person to talk about cutting back dead or dying branches, or about releasing what no longer serves you. I'm the worst at this. I hold on to broken things—literally, relationally, and metaphorically—for way too long. I almost always believe healing is possible. When it comes to looking at my own life for damaged, broken, or dying pieces that need to be pruned and surrendered, I begin by listening for the pain points. Where am I hurting? Where are relational dynamics or belief patterns creating agony? What in my daily life is leading to depression and disconnection from my purpose or deepest values? Once I've identified those points of pain, I then assess whether the pain is constructive or destructive.

Constructive pain is like doing a stretch in yoga that is just beyond your comfort zone, but you know it will build your ability to hold poses for longer. Constructive pain lends itself to bigger goals and aspirations. It's the agony of staying up through the night to meet a writing deadline. It's the discomfort of wading through the relational dysfunction with your partner as you work toward healing. It's the training at the gym to meet your fitness goals. This pain builds something of meaning and value within you. It's the sort of pain that leads to life. In my assessment of the "damaged branches" in my own story, when I encounter pain points that are aligned with the woman I hope to become and with the story I hope to write with my life, I do my best to keep those branches growing even when it's hard and even when it requires a tremendous amount of energy.

Destructive pain, however, is less generative in its function. I know I've crossed the threshold into destructive pain when I've started hiding or keeping secrets from loved ones about how challenging a situation has become, or when there is no pathway to relief or healing in sight and I haven't had the courage to ask for help or direction. Pain can become destructive when we don't take care of a problem early enough in its emergence or when we let a challenging situation go on much longer than it should without correcting course. Destructive pain leads only to greater distress and suffering. I've learned that when such pain crops up in my life due to circumstances created by me, by others, or by the nature of life itself, the best step is to turn to others in vulnerability and ask for help. Inviting others into a painful situation we're living through gives us perspective. Sharing with others helps us discover our options. In my experience, when I'm deep in a painful situation, one that feels destructive and for which I have little hope, telling a few chosen others about the situation opens my eyes to pathways and possibilities I couldn't see before. Pain has a way of narrowing our vision because we're focused on surviving. We need the encouragement of others to lift our heads, to wipe the tears from our eyes, and to make wise choices. When the pain of circumstances becomes destructive, some degree of pruning is necessary.

Setting a firm boundary is a form of pruning. Boundaries are lines we draw to protect, honor, and preserve our own life force and energy so that we can grow toward fruitfulness and well-being. Setting boundaries can help a painful situation shift from being destructive to being constructive. Here are two examples:

- If you have a troubled relationship with alcohol and the habit is creating destructive pain in your life, set a boundary with drinking by cutting back on your alcohol intake. What was once the *destructive* pain of alcohol dependence, through an act of pruning, transforms into the *constructive* pain of leading a life of sobriety. If setting this boundary seems too challenging to do on your own, consider seeking help and support.
- If you are living through a painful season in a relationship for which there seems to be no hope, set boundaries dictating how you will show up in that relationship. Decide what you will and will no longer do in that relationship. Drawing boundaries around your own behavior helps the *destructive* pain of relational dysfunction evolve into the *constructive* pain of self-control and of relating to someone in a new way.

We all have areas in our lives that are damaged. Being a human is difficult. On any given day, a number of scenarios and hardships will bring us to our knees. The upside is that we get to make choices. Like my husband Alex observing the peach and pear trees, we are holding the pruners in our hands. We get to step back, assess which damaged branches need to go, and then, when the time is right, prune.

Pruning What's Distracting Us

Every no we give to one idea, possibility, or priority is a yes we give to another idea, possibility, or priority. When the work of pruning is underway, it's important to remember that every branch cut back is ultimately reinforcing a yes. With every blossom we choose to cut, we're simultaneously making the choice to add life, strength, energy, and creativity to another blossom on its way. This is an energizing aspect of the pruning process. Our decisions, even and especially the costly ones, are never in vain. Once we've removed the damaged branches in our lives, we are then tasked with determining which branches are distractions from the ultimate fruitfulness we've set our sights on.

I often struggle with defining "distraction." As a creative person who is quickly inspired to follow new threads of thought and possibility, I thrive in settings where my mind is able to jump between ideas and where I'm able to draw unexpected connections between seemingly random pieces of information. Sitting in a loud coffee shop while I do my morning journaling is highly energizing to me. There are few things I love more than spending a long, slow morning in the middle of a busy city with paper and a fountain pen in hand. For some, however, sitting in a busy coffee shop with sirens wailing, car horns honking, and people rushing by on the sidewalk outside is hardly enriching. Some find such a setting loud, chaotic, and distressing. What this says to me is that how we define "distraction" is highly personal. Our definitions flow from whatever we've defined as being our focal point or true north. We have to know where we're headed and what our values and priorities are before we can adequately determine what in life draws us away from our predetermined destination.

This is much easier for trees. Their purpose is evident. The focus of a peach tree is to grow peaches. The focus of a pear tree is to grow pears. There is not much doubt or complexity in this for trees. For us mere mortals, however, making determinations about who we are and what we value takes thoughtfulness, nuance, attentiveness, and time. We may not be trees, but we *were* created with intention. Our personalities, gifts, histories, families, and cultures of origin—and the choices we make as individuals—all work together to form a unique expression of personhood. This unique expression looks, sounds, moves, and feels different in each season. Our work is to be as awake as possible to our unique expression so that when it's time to pick up the pruning shears, we know what is calling for our focus and attention and what distractions we need to leave behind. Once we've given name, structure, or form to who we are becoming, we can then define as a distraction any habit of heart, mind, body, or soul that compromises our ability to focus on that trajectory. Distractions are not necessarily damaged or even harmful aspects of our lives. They are simply in the way. Just as cutting the small branches from the peach tree allowed the sunlight to reach deeper into the tree's growing system, cutting out distractions makes room for our energy to flow to the right priorities and places.

Take starting a new business as an example. One of the major milestones in launching a new enterprise is crafting a business plan. In order to craft a business plan, you have to know what your offerings are and you need to have a sense of who your primary customers will be. You also need some measure of time, focus, and creative energy to bring the plan to completion so that you can share it with prospective funders and collaborators. With a well-defined outcome in mind, you can then backtrack to determine what may distract you from reaching this goal.

In my experience, distractions come from both the outside, from forces external to us, and the inside, from our own hearts and minds. Unless you are a full-time entrepreneur with no commitments other than your new project, distractions from the outside will include the responsibilities and roles you must fulfill as a parent, a spouse, a daughter, an auntie, a friend, and so on. We can't easily cut off these relationships, nor should we. But when it comes to completing a task like finishing a business plan, we do have to set boundaries and communicate our priorities to those around us. This is the work of pruning and managing the flow of energy in our lives.

In my life, pruning looks like taking off from work on Fridays so that I have dedicated time during the week to plan. Outside distractions that are easier to prune include things like social media and entertainment. These distractions tend to drain mental, emotional, and creative energy away from the task at hand. In these cases, the work of pruning is to negotiate boundaries around these external forces. This looks like removing applications like Instagram and YouTube from my phone so that I'm not tempted to get lost in a content binge or a scrolling loop when I ought to be creating.

Pruning distractions from the inside is a much more challenging endeavor. Distractions from the inside are patterns of thought that crop up and make a lot of noise, especially when we set our sights on becoming fruitful and expressive in a new way. These inner distractions send messages like "Who do you think you are creating this new business?" and "No one is going to care what you have to offer." Inner distractions often reinforce the most challenging lies we confront on any given day: "You are wasting your time trying to make your mark on the world" and "You don't deserve this opportunity." I am learning that pruning these inner distractions is just like pruning a fruit tree: You wait for the right season, you assess what's really going on, and then you cut these distractions from your life.

Here is one practice that works for me when a big and noisy inner distraction pops up. If a thought is ruminating, I slow my breathing and I speak the thought aloud or I write it down.

Something about speaking it out loud or writing it down helps me create distance between the thought and myself. Once I've created some distance, which can take anywhere from thirty seconds to a few days depending on the magnitude of the thought, I then ask myself a series of questions: Is this true? What evidence do I have of this being true? Who told me this? What evidence do I have to the contrary? If this thought is true, what can I do to create a new reality through my future actions and choices? Over time, through this process of intentional reflection, these inner distractions transform from noisy detractors to voices of insight and empowerment.

Over and over again, I've found that even my most critical and challenging inner distractions are aspects of myself wanting to keep me safe from disappointment, loss, or harm. They mean well, even if their tactics create emotional distress. One of my goals recently has been to nurture self-confidence in my body, and one of the inner distractions that often speaks up is especially critical. This inner voice critiques my dietary choices, my wardrobe decisions, and even my levels of activity on any given day. When these thoughts come to mind, I turn toward them with my inner gaze and I say something along the lines of "Thank you for trying to push me toward my goals. I want you to know that your criticism isn't helping me, though I appreciate your efforts. Know that I will love my body into health and vitality; I will not shame it." These gentle conversations with the more critical and distracting parts of myself are a pruning practice. This is my way of attending to these inner distractions and trimming them back so that they no longer siphon off my energy. This work has taken years of practice, but I am reaping a harvest of self-compassion on the other side. If you struggle with managing the inner distractions in your life, what might it look like to take time to reflect, assess what's there, and enter into conversation with those distractions so that they can be transformed from distractions into gifts?

Pruning What's Beyond Our Capacity to Hold

We prune what's been damaged and broken beyond repair. We prune what distracts us, both outside and inside, from becoming who we are meant to be. Lastly, we're invited to prune whatever is beyond our capacity to hold. We're invited to cultivate a confident and sturdy no. Why? So that when we bump into our limits, we are empowered with the fortitude and perspective to draw boundaries, communicate our needs, and confidently draw our energy back to what's manageable for us.

When driving down the long gravel pathway to my parents' farm, visitors are always met by two large peach trees planted in the middle of the cattle field just to the left of the driveway. Pear and plum trees are planted there too, but they're much younger and smaller. The peach trees are older, stronger, more firmly planted, and they deliver the sweetest summer peaches—the kind Georgia is famous for. Unlike my brother's fruit trees, however, my parents' peach trees were not pruned last winter. When summertime came, there was an abundance of fruit growing for harvest, so much so that one of the tree's largest branches snapped during a windy storm. The weight of the fruit was so heavy that the branch wasn't strong enough to weather the storm. The branch snapped, compromising the tree's present and future fruitfulness, at least for a time.

When we welcome the pruning shears into our lives, it's not only to cut away the damaged and the distracting. We also have to say no to good things in order to make sure that we have the strength to stand under the weight of our lives' fruitfulness. Determining what good things in our lives to cut is among the toughest decisions we make. This is especially true for those of us who are oriented toward achievement and who enjoy the novelty of more and more and more. The work of pruning calls us to less but better. Less but *deeper*. It is countercultural work.

One of the greatest myths pulsing beneath the surface of modern life tells us, "You can have it all." You can be the best at home and at work. You can be a fully engaged parent, daughter, spouse, employee, and friend—all at one time. You can make plenty of money, build a stellar investment portfolio, and give to your church and to charity while having enough to drive the best car and wear whatever brands you find most attractive. You can have it all. You can do it all and be it all, and it will cost you little to nothing. There are no boundaries and no limits. "Shoot for the moon," they say, "and you'll land among the stars." Since when did being grounded, here with our feet on the earth and in wholehearted embrace of all that is within our hearts' and arms' reach, prove not to be enough?

Even if you consciously know this myth to be a lie, our culture is saturated with lofty expectations of achieving the impossible. This is the story we glean from our movies, our magazines, and our social media feeds. Let us not forget the promised joy and satisfaction ever dangling on the end of a thread in front of us, constantly drawing us in, constantly asking for just a little bit more—more effort, more energy, more time. "Just keep working," the myth says, "and one day you will finally feel as if you have everything you want and need."

The pressure created by these unrealistic expectations does a number on the soul. The pressure compels us to push, to contort, even to malform our inner lives and our outer selves to fit a narrative of seeming perfection and achievement. Is it exhausting? Of course. Is it worth it? The myth says so. How do we get off modernity's conveyor belt moving toward excess and striving? How might we orient ourselves toward true abundance, found in contentment, gratitude, and acceptance of what is? How do we say no to the myth and its promises and instead live in a more honest and rooted way?

We let go. We welcome the pruning. We cut off, cut back, set boundaries, and say no. We release the old way by shedding the stories we once held close. While it can be challenging to let go of our expectations of productivity and achievement, there is also a freedom in being honest enough to say, "This pressure is crushing me." There is a relief that rushes in when we trim back even the strongest branches in our lives, knowing that we are making a decision that will carry forth health and abundance for years to come.

I've been reckoning with this idea of pruning *good* things and *good* desires for the sake of honoring the limits of my life, specifically as it relates to my remaining childfree into my mid-thirties. For the longest time, I believed that to be fully woman and fully alive, I needed to get pregnant, birth a baby, and raise a family. I believed this specific vision was the only way to actualize a truly meaningful and fulfilling life. However, by God's grace, I've been coming home more and more to the reality that biological motherhood may not be in the cards for me. While I've had times of disappointment around this, what is also true is that I find it increasingly liberating to release the pressure I've felt to validate my womanhood in this particular way. Slowly and beautifully, with true help from the heavens, I have been pruning these inner narratives, many of which are filled with narrow definitions of what it means to be a woman. With each snip of the pruning shears, I find myself freer. I am freer in my body. I am freer in my dreams for the future. I am freer in my relationships with others. I am freer to say yes to the life that is in front of me instead of attempting to force a life I was told would make me happy. It is the sweetest liberation I've known to date. My life remains just as fertile and fruitful as ever.

The invitation here is to assess what you have the capacity to carry in this season. What good things are you being invited to surrender? What good dreams need to be trimmed back or released for a time? What emotions arise as you contemplate this letting go? It is not easy to let the sun set on the ideas, possibilities, and dreams you've carried in your heart. It's tough to say no or not right now. But as you work within your limits and as you dance with whatever each season brings, day by day, you'll find that surrendering the old way is the exact release your life needs to grow.

Saying Yes to the Process

One of the most striking observations I made while watching Alex prune my brother's fruit trees that day was how the task called for Alex's full-body investment. He had to climb up into the tree to reach the branches for their removal. He had to trust his body to hold him in balance while also trusting the strength of the larger branches to keep him from falling. He moved methodically and wisely, reaching back to the ladder every now and then to recalibrate before venturing back into the tree's growing system of bare branches. He seemed to move with the tree, becoming part of it in a way. His movement through the tree, his tending to it with such thoughtfulness and care, was a little bit of magic.

When we come to a pruning moment, when we stand back and look at our lives for what needs repair and release, the process calls for a full-body investment. The process calls for us to climb even more deeply into the crevices of our inner lives with curiosity, attentiveness, and care. This is not work we can do well in the midst of hurried and busy days. Proactively stewarding our lives is often inconvenient. The gift of saying yes to this reflective and decisive work is that we learn how to live life with intention. We do not control outcomes; we cannot control outcomes. We can, however, create conditions for flourishing.

Welcoming the pruning shears is about saying yes to the imperfect process of your own formation. It's getting into the details of how you work and of how your history is shaping your worldview. It's learning to be open and clear about what your values are and about what honest living means to you. To welcome the pruning shears is to actively respond to the ways your life is calling you to heal and mature. It is the work of taking initiative, making plans, and becoming the head gardener of your own life.

I spent years wanting something outside me to climb up into the branches of my life and save me from all my insecurity and doubts. I outsourced my soul's formation to church, to school, to bosses, to romantic partners, and more. It wasn't until I picked up the pruning shears and prayerfully began cutting away old beliefs, destructive habits, harmful distractions, and anything I was too tired to keep holding on to that I began experiencing a sort of fruitfulness that sustains. Of course, this is an ever-evolving process, and I'm confident the future holds new lessons for me. Even still, if you feel stuck as you're actualizing a more beautiful way of living, I invite you to pick up your pruning shears and to begin the patient, diligent work of pruning.

A Note About Grieving

Pruning, even the necessary and chosen kind, carries grief in its wake. Grief is that swirling mixture of deep love and deep loss held together in our spirits as we say goodbye to what cannot come with us along our path. Nature itself has a way of reminding me that both yesterday's trials and yesterday's triumphs will soon be in the wind. Like sand slipping through my fingers, time keeps moving forward, and my attempts to grasp and control prove futile. Leaving the city to make a home in a slower place was the medicine I needed at the time, but like all good medicine, it had a bitter taste. Moving from one version of my life to another called me to grieve all the damaged, distracting, and good but weighty responsibilities I was leaving behind.

I've never been great at goodbyes. I think back to my first few weeks after college graduation. While I'd said "goodbye" and "so long" to my friends, something in me still believed life would feel just as connected and rich following our dispersal across the world as it had while we were all together on campus each day. My heart moved through the grief slowly as I sought to build a life in a new community right away. Looking back now, I don't think I grieved that change at all. I just kept moving, stuffing down the sadness and disappointment while working hard to prove myself worthy in a new environment. While graduation was a welcomed and celebrated transition, I didn't know my body and soul needed a process to release what was and to formally acknowledge that such a sweet season was over.

Grief has a way of lodging itself in the flesh and organs within. It has a way of resting gently, like a weighted blanket, applying pressure to our souls and inviting us to be honest about all we love and all we've lost. We grieve not only the people who come and go like waves over the years of our lives but also the versions of ourselves we once were. We grieve the dreams whose time came and went; we grieve the dreams we held in heart and mind but never got the chance to hold in our arms. We grieve the stories we hoped would be true. Grief comes and, like a good massage therapist, applies the exact amount of pressure our bodies and souls need to tell the truth. To say the honest words stuck in the back of our throats. To lament, to weep, to wail. Grief invites us to honor the love we hold. If we ignore grief's invitations, the pressure increases. This is not to cause harm but to help heal. Grief keeps us soft, pliable, and tender and invites us ever more deeply into the textures of what it means to be a person: one who is animated by Love itself.

Welcoming the pruning shears is a way of also welcoming grief and goodbyes. We open our hands, surrendering control, hoping and praying that the changes we've made are worth it.

There are no guarantees. We cannot know what storms will come, which branches will bear fruit, and which branches will snap under the pressure. We cannot know how the story will end. We can, however, pay close attention, pick up the pruning shears, and do our very best to create the conditions for good and beautiful things to grow.

PAUSE & REFLECT

Our work in part 2 has been about cultivation. Cultivation is the work of getting into the gardens of our lives, sowing new seeds, pulling old weeds, and building our capacity to create an inner life that is able to sustain an outer life of groundedness, peace, presence, and connection. It is countercultural work. Urgency, anxiety, and scatteredness are the norm. This work you're doing—embracing slow time, caring for your body, attending to your inner terrain, living with the seasons, listening for your longings, and making room for new growth through pruning—will enable you to become a non-anxious, firmly rooted presence in a chaotic and often overwhelming world.

As I think back to why I began living a more beautiful way, I see that so much of me was simply longing to feel safe and at home in my body. I was craving margin to know myself more deeply and to connect with others more authentically. I was in a lot of pain from having spent so much time trying to do and be everything I thought others wanted me to do and be. I was in a wilderness, and I felt lost. Integrating the practices listed above gave me the emotional capacity and nourishment I needed to finally take ownership of my own story, to set needed boundaries, to take risks for what mattered most to me, and to walk away from anything that didn't make for more life and flourishing. This doesn't mean I stopped facing difficult things; I'm still walking through difficult things. What this does mean is that cultivating a more beautiful way has given me the resources I need so that I can face those challenges with courage, focus, and self-control. With practice, and in time, I hope the same is true for you.

Here are a few questions to deepen your reflections on the themes of part 2.

On Living with the Seasons

1. Is living with the seasons an accessible practice for you? If yes, how? If no, why not?
2. How would you describe your relationship with the natural world?
3. Which of the four seasons (autumn, winter, spring, summer) best reflects the current season happening in your inner terrain? Why?

On Listening for Your Longings

1. What energizes you about identifying your longings? What, if anything, drains you about identifying your longings?
2. Name one pain point or difficult situation you're currently living through. What are you learning in the midst of this challenging experience?
3. Who are the people who help you make decisions? What do you find helpful about their presence, partnership, or advice?

On Making Room for New Growth

1. Think of a time when you had to let something go in order to make room for something new. What was that

experience like? What did you learn about yourself and about life?

2. What in your life is currently distracting you from pursuing the longings or priorities you've identified for yourself?
3. How would you describe your relationship to grief? What has grief taught you?

INTERMISSION

I stepped outside on a cold winter morning and was greeted by clear skies, frost on the earth, bare trees, and a lone birdsong echoing off in the distance. I breathed deeply. I was cold but grateful and totally at home in my skin. I held my coffee mug in both hands as I reveled in the perfection of this chilly, quiet start to the day. *It's been four years since that visit to the emergency room*, I thought to myself. *What a new life I'm living now.*

This was my life: Alex and I had been living in our little black barn house for a couple of years now. We added two dogs into the mix. I was working for myself from my home office. My days were filled with meetings and good work, but I had the space to care for my body first. And while conflict still showed up in my relationships, and while periods of anxiety about work or the state of the world still kept me up at night, I was grateful. I knew that even on my worst days, I had the skills necessary to find my way back home to myself and to the beautiful way I'd started paving all those years prior.

This journey of nurturing a grounded, soul-nourishing life in which I'm learning to receive and accept life as it comes has taught me that every step of the way is worth trying. Embracing slow time is worth trying because urgency is able to reproduce only itself. Connecting with your body is worth trying because leading a life of disassociation and disconnection, over the long haul, only creates more pain. Awakening to your inner terrain is worth trying because it's among the best ways to stop living reactively to the chaos spinning all around you. Learning how to live with the seasons is worth trying because it lends itself to good outcomes for almost every other living creature on the planet. Listening for your longings is worth trying because it's the only way to make sure the life you're leading is really and truly your own, springing up from the unique gifts of your own story and soul. Lastly, making room for new growth is worth trying because doing so ensures that you have the time, energy, and resources to devote to what matters most.

As we turn the corner toward the last part of this book, I want to celebrate how far you've come. A more beautiful way to live is available to you, and the practices you've encountered thus far will support you in making this way real.

Part 3 is all about how to sustain this way of being. We sustain it through rituals, by opening our hearts to the world, and by letting beauty lead us. Let's journey on.

PART THREE

SUSTENANCE

Seven

NOURISHING YOUR LIFE THROUGH RITUALS

I'd never been to a vespers service before. I walked into the church, and all my senses were instantly captivated. I quietly observed, taking it all in—the smell of incense moving across the room, the sounds of bells and of the choir chanting Scriptures, the yellow glow of candlelight illuminating the faces of saints from centuries past. I was stunned and fully engaged in the moment. I'd never seen anything quite like it. It was as though I'd been transported into an alternate, holy universe where time was standing still and we, together, were gazing upon the eternal. It was remarkable.

I wasn't looking for a new church or faith community, as I'd been without one for some time and was quite content with the patchwork spiritual life I'd created. A little bit of Scripture here, a little bit of spiritual direction there, and a whole lot of journaling and time in nature. Alex, however, had been holding a curiosity about the Eastern Orthodox Church for some time, and he'd started attending services every so often. Out of a desire to understand what he was experiencing, I decided to tag along to a vespers service one Wednesday night. Not only was the service beautiful, but it also struck a deep chord in me about the importance of ritual and of having dedicated time and space to step out of our lives and into practices that draw us toward our higher values.

The weekly rituals of vespers and liturgy in the Eastern Orthodox Church ground the faithful in a life wholly oriented around the person of Jesus Christ and around what it means to be his church. The belief is that, as you participate in the rituals of the faith community, especially over an extended period of time, your inner life and your outer life begin to conform to the values and priorities set forth by that community. I liken it to being a rock in a river of water. The community and its rituals are the river. The person who steps into that community is the rock. Over time, the rituals soften, shape, and smooth the rock's edges. This gentle work of refinement, moving us toward our values, is the gift that rituals offer us.

We can also see rituals as vessels. They are a means of moving us from one state of being to another. By incorporating daily, weekly, monthly, and annual rituals of attentiveness, calmness, and connection into our lives, we will find that what once felt nearly impossible to do—like slowing down—will eventually become our new normal and will last over time.

Rituals are often associated with religious practice. The technical definition speaks of rites and ceremonies and of religious law.[1] But rituals are so much more than all that formal religious tradition holds. Rituals are personal customs and communal norms we observe consistently and repeatedly over time. It is in this consistency and repetition that our hearts, minds, and souls are formed. Not quickly but gently. Not hurriedly but methodically. Not fearfully but steadily. Rituals are integral to living a more beautiful way because they help us mark time, they involve the various faculties of our bodies, and they shape our souls.

I suspect that if you were to step back and look at your life, you'd see that it's littered with rituals, big and small, each and every day. You may even be able to delineate between the rituals that are adding value to your life and those that seem to be stealing from you. When I think of the valuable rituals in my life, my mind goes to the "good mornings" exchanged between my husband and me each day and to the sound of dog food as it lands in my pups' bowls for their morning meal. I think of my daily moment to sit at my desk and journal with a beloved fountain pen or my afternoon phone call with my mom. These are the little rituals—my own tiny ceremonies—that keep me tethered to who I am and who I love.

If I'm honest, however, there are also the rituals that function like little thieves, stealing my attention, my sense of calm, and my energy. There's the ritual of checking my email as soon as I wake up, filling my mind with whatever morning news dispatch wants my immediate focus. There's the almost hourly ritual of checking my social media feeds and email inbox for whatever priorities the world wants to set for me in any given moment. Over the years, there have also been more destructive rituals, like a daily "wine down" of sauvignon blanc, despite knowing that too much wine before bed makes for poor sleep and a sluggish start to the next day.

These are just a handful of the daily rituals I could name for myself, and I imagine you would have quite the list if you were to do the same. What's worth noting here is how all the rituals mentioned above, as small as they may be, if practiced consistently and repeatedly, generate specific outcomes in life. Daily connection with loved ones makes for a life of connection to loved ones. Daily onslaughts of frenetic, distressing news make for a heart that is frenetic and distressed. This is the simple power of rituals. They make or break a life.

Living a more beautiful way is sustained through rituals. Given the way rituals form us over time, as you prioritize the daily, weekly, monthly, and annual practices we will discuss, you will awaken to a whole new way of being. You won't be able to stay the same. The routines I'm offering here are not exhaustive. They are the ones I personally return to again and again as I seek to sustain this way of living in my neck of the woods.

Daily Rituals

We begin with daily rituals because they are often the most accessible. They are the ones you can begin practicing quickly, and they are often the easiest to adjust as you have need. You can truly make these your own. The two daily rituals I recommend are slow time and movement.

Slow Time

As you may recall from part 1, slow time is any moment you choose to be fully present to the reality of your life. Slow time is an opportunity to spend a specific block of time in prayer, journaling, meditation, or self-reflection. This time block can be anything from fifteen minutes to an hour. The goal of this time is to check in with yourself, to name how you're doing, to listen for your longings and needs, and to honor whatever emotions, hopes, anxieties, or fears are present.

One of my favorite activities for slow time is stream-of-consciousness journaling. This idea was popularized by Julia Cameron, author of *The Artist's Way*.[2] She encourages people to write, by hand, three pages of their stream of consciousness. This is a freewriting process with no editing. You simply write. I love this practice because whatever is inside of me—happy, fearful, energizing, or sad—has a place on the page.

If writing or journaling feels intimidating to you, you can use your slow time to read Scripture or poetry. You can sit in silence and listen to the world around you. You can complete a body scan to check in and see how you're doing. You can fill this time however you like. The goal is to practice pausing, being attentive to your inner life, and cultivating presence and self-awareness.

Slow time can also be a dedicated time in your day to rest. It can look like sitting in the sun. It can look like spending twenty minutes in silence before you go to bed. It can look like taking a nap. Taking a daily break to rest from your life's work, whatever it entails, is a way to ritualize slow time.

By engaging in this practice daily, you not only build your capacity to prioritize slow time and to enjoy it but also put into practice skills of self-awareness and reflection that you can use throughout the rest of your day. For example, if you take time to journal about a challenging situation in a relationship, you increase the likelihood that you'll be able to communicate more effectively because you've done the work to name what's going on inside you. In this instance, by spending slow time attending to your inner world, you set yourself up to interact with others more thoughtfully. Slow time not only empowers you in the moment but also equips you to remain emotionally and spiritually engaged as the day goes on.

Movement

Daily movement is a ritual for honoring our bodies. Movement offers us numerous benefits that have a holistic, positive impact on us. Movement helps our bodies and spirits process emotions. It physically strengthens us, literally adding years to our lives and life to our years. Movement also has the ability to bring clarity and focus to our minds, allowing us to shake off the haziness we might experience on occasion.

In recent months, I went through a particularly stressful season in my new job. While I'd been living a more beautiful way for a few years, life was still happening, as it does, and I was doing my best to weather the storm. During this stressful time, I found myself daydreaming about riding a bike.

Biking is all I wanted to do. I hadn't owned a bike in years, but something about the idea of coasting along my street filled me with a sense of freedom and excitement. I just wanted to ride. After mentioning this to Alex over and over again, we decided it was time to get a bike. We did some research on nearby shops, hopped in the car, and within a few hours I was back home, on my wheels, riding free and fully alive down our street.

Being able to move my body in this way didn't make all my work challenges disappear, but the movement lifted my spirits. The movement gave me momentum. It sparked possibility in my soul and helped me generate ways to solve the challenges in front of me. Movement is powerful in its ability to shake things up and help us know our own strength.

Your body's wisdom is a gift, and movement keeps you in tune with your body's experience. I cannot be too prescriptive here, though, because our bodies are different, as are their limits, abilities, and needs. What works for one of us will not necessarily work for another. What I can offer is that daily movement—whether you go for a walk, strength train at a gym, chase your toddler around the living room, or do gentle exercises at your desk—is one way you can consistently nourish connection with your body. Then when it's time to check in on how you're doing, what you need, and what might need to change for you to live more fully in the here and now, you're already dialed in to what your body might have to say.

Weekly Rituals

Weekly rituals are practiced at least once every seven days. You can approach them in at least one of two ways: You can wait until you've gotten the daily rituals under your belt before you fold in a weekly ritual, or you can forgo the daily rituals and prioritize the weekly ones instead. For some, daily rituals are more accessible, but for others, setting aside intentional time on a weekly basis is much more realistic. Know that you can be flexible here and that you have options. The two weekly rituals I recommend are community and play.

Community

Much of our focus for living a more beautiful way has been on the individual. This is by design. My working theory is that as individual people cultivate an inner life of groundedness, presence, and resilience in the face of all the challenges life brings, the ripple effect of their influence will be more groundedness, presence, and resilience in the world. As with fractals, what becomes true for the smallest unit of humanity—the individual person—has the chance to become true for humanity as a whole. While I believe this wholeheartedly, sustaining this way of living is a collective endeavor. We cannot do it on our own. We need friends, teachers, companions, encouragers, and so many guides along the way.

Community offers us two gifts: refinement and encouragement. Community refines us by fostering scenarios in which who we are and what we value bump up against who other people are and what they value. In this encounter with the other, we must grapple with the discomfort and difficulty of being in relationships with people who act, think, feel, believe, and live differently than we do. This friction has the possibility to refine our character, to build our communication skills, and to expand our capacity to love. Community is the testing ground for a more beautiful way. If you can remain settled and calm only when you're interacting with people who think just like you do, then your practice of a more beautiful way is stifled. If you can learn how to remain rooted and at home in who you are as you nurture relationships in diverse community, then you're well on your path toward living a more beautiful way that may very well transform the world.

The second gift of community is encouragement. It is good to have regular points of meaningful contact with people who will champion your desire to create a non-anxious life. Along this path you will encounter internal and external roadblocks that will keep you from moving forward. You will take one step in the direction you want to go, life will happen, and you may very well end up two or three steps back. Community keeps you going. Friends hold you when the pain is way too much. Faith leaders inspire you when you feel like giving up. Teachers and guides offer you perspective and insight to help you make sense of your experience. A spiritual community holds your biggest questions and reminds you that you are loved.

Building community and meaningful connections with people is not easy, so if this feels out of reach to you for whatever reason, start really small. Is there a friend you can have a weekly phone call with? Is there a local coffee shop you can commit to visiting for one hour each week in order to meet new people? Is there a regular gathering of a religious or spiritual community you can begin attending? Be intentional and start small.

Play

Fun and delight give us energy, spark our imaginations, and fill us with laughter and joy. In a way, play is also incredibly vulnerable, as we must feel safe and secure enough to open our hearts and to let down our protective shields of seriousness, productivity, and the need to be in control. When I think of what this vulnerability is like, my dog Bear comes to mind. He's a seventy-pound, three-year-old lab mix. His bark is deep and loud. He is stubborn and tremendously strong. If you didn't know any better, you'd think he was the most serious pup around. However, as is true for many of his breed, he's a big lover of snuggles and playtime. He lives to chase tennis balls and to chew on sticks. One of his favorite ways to play is to roll over on his back for a good belly rub. He just lies there, fully disarmed and immersed in the moment of connection and delight. Similarly, play is a chance for us to disarm, to be soft and receptive, and to let ourselves feel the joy of being alive.

Weekly play is a dedicated time and space to have fun, to create, and to enjoy being a human. Prioritizing play does not come easily for me, nor does it for most of the overachievers I know. This is why we make play a ritual—a regular practice that moves us from focusing on our seriousness and pain and invites us to lean instead into our levity and glee. Here are a few ways to integrate play into your weekly schedule:

- Engage in playtime with pets or children. I know this may not be for everyone, but for some, intentional play with the little ones or the beloved animals in their lives reminds them of what it looks like to embrace simplicity, delight, and imagination. For many children, and pets for that matter, getting into play mode is as easy as breathing. In their presence, we are reminded of what it's like to be carefree for a time.
- Return to hobbies or playtime activities you enjoyed as a kid. Go on a bike ride, put a puzzle together, play a board game, or complete some arts and crafts. Remember that play is about enjoyment, not performance. As a girl, I loved paper and scrapbooking. Over the past couple of years, I have returned to my love for stationery and have been building a collection of notebooks, writing utensils, stickers, and more, all for the love of it. I set aside time each week to do creative journaling, to clean my fountain pens, and to write handwritten notes to the people who've impacted me that week. It's been a life-giving hobby that brings gladness and pleasure to my days.
- Join a sports league, go to a trivia night, or show up to a comedy show. These are all communal activities that

have the potential to draw you out of the seriousness of your life and into the magic of it. Communal playtime activities are also special because they remind us that we are not alone in our need to feel alive.

Much of living a more beautiful way is about the important, and at times serious, work of cultivating awareness so that we can make decisions from a place that feels firmly planted and within ourselves. This work is challenging and good. But every so often, we have to be able to come up for air after doing all this deep, thoughtful soul work. If we don't prioritize playtime, laughter, and sheer happiness, we may very well miss some of the beauty our lives hold. We don't heal just to mitigate the pain in our lives; we also heal so that we have the capacity to embrace the elation. Weekly play is a ritual that prepares our hearts to receive joy when it comes.

Monthly Rituals

Monthly rituals are openings for us to step back and reflect on big-picture themes. As a culture, we mark time according to a monthly calendar, and much of our lives is arranged around these twelve movements of time. While daily and weekly rituals assist us with being more alive to the moment right in front of us, monthly rituals help us look back on the past and set intentions for the future. The two monthly rituals I offer you are spiritual direction and gratitude.

Spiritual Direction

Spiritual direction has become an anchor practice in my life, as it is one space I can reliably go where I know my whole story will be received with care and love. There is something holy and otherworldly about reflecting on my life as though it were a rich, sacred text. In spiritual direction, I've processed grief as

I've moved through changes in my faith life. I've found support as I've navigated evolutions in my racial identity. I've learned how to listen to my inner voice, when to follow its wisdom and when to give it boundaries. I've experienced emotional healing, spiritual renewal, and professional clarity all from having a dedicated time and space for my life to be witnessed, honored, and held by a faithful companion.

Spiritual direction typically takes the form of a one-on-one session with a trained spiritual care practitioner who holds space for you and helps you listen for the movements, shifts, and wisdom bubbling up from within your deepest self. A spiritual director asks questions, reflects back to you what they're hearing you say, and with your consent draws your attention to how the divine is at work in your story. As we move through life, there are times when we're tasked with making meaning of our circumstances, but as when standing two inches away from a portrait hanging in a museum, we're just too close to see the big picture. By entering into the texture of your life with a companion whose only job is to bear witness and offer support, you're able to take some steps back and see things more clearly. They help you notice, pay attention to, and align your actions with your values.

Additionally, I recommend spiritual direction as a monthly ritual because the sessions become opportunities for you to practice the activities explored in this book. A spiritual direction session is an exercise in embracing slow time, in noticing the sensations of your body, and in awakening to what's happening within your inner terrain. Spiritual direction is also a place where you can further develop how to live with the seasons, how to listen for your longings, and how to make room for new growth. All the practices of a more beautiful way to live are honed and reinforced through spiritual direction.

If you don't know where to find a spiritual director, you can visit the website of Spiritual Directors International and search the directory.[3]

Gratitude

When I was a college student, I had very low self-esteem. I'm not sure if this is true for all twenty-year-olds, but it was very true for me. I became aware of this condition of my soul through a conversation with a dear friend. He'd been listening to me talk, and while I don't remember what we were discussing, I do remember him asking me point blank, "Bethaney, do you think you have to earn people's love?" My eyes filled with tears instantly. "Yes, I think so." He looked at me with sincerity and care before saying, "That's not true." We sat in silence for a moment, knowing that something holy and unexpected had just passed between us. It was a sacred moment, one I will never forget.

Days later I reached out to my pastor, because I wanted to keep exploring what my friend and I had unearthed in that short exchange. We met for coffee at a local shop, and my pastor gently and graciously held space for me to unwind what my friend and I had discussed. After I told him the story, he asked me, "Bethaney, if you were to survey one hundred people about yourself and ninety-nine of the responses were amazing and one was negative, which category of responses do you think you'd be most focused on?" I responded without hesitation, "Oh, I'd be focused on the one. I'd want to know why they felt the way they did, and I'd want to see what I could do to change their mind."

While this exchange happened fifteen years ago, and I've been on an illuminating trajectory of building self-esteem ever since, it was a powerful lesson for me about the role negativity bias plays in our lives. Negativity bias refers to the human tendency not only to register negative stimuli more easily but also to dwell on negative things for longer periods of time than we dwell on positive things.[4] While many factors led to my low self-esteem, I do think negativity bias played a role. It was easier for me to focus on my perceived failures than my achievements. It was easier to fix my gaze on what I lacked than what I had to offer. It was normal for me to emphasize what I believed I was doing wrong instead of having appreciation for all I was doing right.

Gratitude is a ritual for living a more beautiful way because it teaches our hearts, minds, and souls how to see and celebrate the good and the beautiful all around us and within us. Expressing appreciation for ourselves and the gifts in our lives reminds us of our worth. Gratitude has a mending influence on our spirits and a balm-like effect on wounded and worried hearts. It is an antidote to negativity bias and, with practice, generates within us a worldview of possibility, creativity, and hope.

It is tempting to disregard the potency of a gratitude practice because it's so simple. You set aside time to take note of what you're grateful for, of what is working, and of all that is worthy of celebration. Gratitude can be a daily, weekly, or monthly task, but I've placed it here as a monthly ritual because it's a chance to reflect on an entire month of your life and to give thanks. You can make a list in your journal. You can sit quietly and name the items you're grateful for to yourself, one at a time. You can make a communal celebration by gathering with friends and sharing your gratitude lists with one another. What might a monthly gratitude practice look like for you?

Gratitude is a ritual for sustaining a more beautiful way because we need moments to acknowledge how far we've come and to feel gratefulness for how we've grown. I look back on that dear twenty-year-old version of myself, and I love her. I know she was doing the best she could with the tools she had, and I believe if she could see how brave, confident, and self-assured I feel today, she'd be so proud. Acknowledging how far you've come will inspire you to keep going as you make this more beautiful way of living your own.

Annual Rituals

Lastly, we practice annual rituals that may be more challenging to do on a daily, weekly, or monthly schedule. These rituals compel us to draw from the depths of our lives. They require a degree of spaciousness and emotional energy. They may even cost money, which requires saving and planning to ensure we have the financial capacity to invest in time away. I offer these annual rituals because without them we run the risk of getting stuck in the past or of losing sight of the future we're living toward. The two annual rituals I commend are letting go and dreaming.

Letting Go

We've explored the necessity of pruning, of shedding, of releasing all that cannot come with us as we create a more grounded and present life. We don't shed just one time; we shed countless times. In leaving a scattered, anxious way of being behind, we release not only jobs, relationships, and places. We also release old belief systems, dysfunctional emotional patterns, and harmful ways of thinking and behaving. Over time, as we evolve, we must embrace the ongoing invitation to let go. We can ritualize our letting go by setting aside an intentional time, at least once a year, to shed our outdated stories and beliefs and to offer gratitude for the lessons letting go has brought into our lives. To this end, below is a ritual for letting go that you can adopt as needed. I recommend reading through the entire ritual at least once before you begin.

Gather the following supplies: a writing utensil, paper, scissors, and a candle.

Find a comfortable place in your home or outdoors. Choose somewhere you feel safe, trusting, and held. You can sit on the floor if that feels grounding for you, but sitting at a table or desk works just as well.

Light a candle as a symbol, marking this moment as sacred time.

Settle in. Let your senses calm. Soften your gaze or close your eyes. Rest in this state for a moment or two.

When you're ready, cut a piece of paper into six to eight strips. The strips need to be large enough for you to write a few words, up to a sentence, on each one. Once you have the strips, respond to the following questions by writing an answer on each strip of paper:

What am I releasing? What am I being invited to let go?

What lessons have I learned from these pieces of my life?

What pain am I looking forward to leaving behind?

What gifts am I hoping to receive in this letting go?

Take note in a journal or mentally of any thoughts, ideas, images, or impressions that come to mind. Then reflect on what you wrote on the strips of paper, offering a few words of gratitude for each thing you're releasing. For example, "Thank you for the gifts you've given me. Thank you for the growth you've brought into my life. Our time has come to an end, but I will carry your wisdom with me."

When you're finished offering gratitude, make plans to release the pieces of paper in a way you find nourishing. If I'm outside and it's safe to do so, I like to burn the pieces of paper in a small firesafe jar and then sprinkle the ashes in the woods. I have also cut the strips of paper into small pieces, like confetti, before immersing them in a bowl of water to dissolve. You can also cut the pieces smaller and recycle them. The choice is yours.

When the process is done, sit in silence for a few minutes. You can respond in prayer or with a poem and then move into the rest of your day.

It is important to note that sometimes this process is emotional. Other times it is not emotional at all. The goal is not emotional expression but to acknowledge our goodbyes, to give voice to the wisdom our experiences carry, and to move forward in gratitude for whatever gifts letting go may bring.

Dreaming

The last ritual for sustaining a more beautiful way of living involves going to a mountaintop. By this I mean going to a place where your heart soars, where you're inspired, and where you're able to dream. It doesn't have to be a literal mountaintop, but it is important that you break away from your normal routine and prioritize presence in a place that lifts you up, recharges your energy, and refreshes your spirit.

A few years into living a more beautiful way for myself, I had the pleasure of going on a writing retreat in central Mexico. I gathered with a community of women I'd never met before, and together we broke open our hearts and our stories as we shared from the depths of who we are. We wrote poetry and prose. We read our art aloud. We dined, we wept, we laughed. We enjoyed ourselves and one another. What was so striking about the timing of this retreat was that I was living through a very painful season in one of my closest relationships. I couldn't see myself or my reality very clearly. Pain has a way of blurring our vision, and I was stuck. However, leaving home, flying to a new place, interacting with strangers and their gorgeous souls, and exercising creative muscles I had previously neglected all worked together to dislodge me from the painful thought loops I'd been stuck in. This mountaintop experience gave me energy and perspective. I came back to daily life with renewed vision. I remembered my identity, my purpose, and my worth because I took a moment away from my everyday life to dream again.

If you are to sustain a more beautiful way to live, you must find your mountaintop and prioritize going there at least once per year. You'll need the energy. You'll need the vision. You'll need the reminders of who you are and what you're worth. A grounded life is not a life void of struggle; it is a life you till and tend, hoe and mend. You'll have to nourish and invest in it every step of the way. An annual ritual of getting away and creating space to dream will give you direction, inspiration, and momentum for when life brings difficulties and disappointments.

One Day at a Time

The various rituals I've offered here are a few of many possibilities. I encourage you to try the ones that seem exciting or especially feasible for you in this season. Start there and check in every few months or so to determine what adjustments you'd like to make to sustain these practices for the long haul.

The journey you'll take from leading an urgent, worried life to leading a more tethered life of attentiveness and self-awareness will not happen overnight. Learning how to live a more beautiful way unfolds over years. There will be years of breakthrough and healing. There will be years of discouragement and heartache. There will be years that change your mind about everything you think you know and believe about being human. The best you can do is take life one day at a time while incorporating the rituals and practices that strengthen and enliven you along the way.

Eight

OPENING YOUR HEART TO THE WORLD

For years I believed I would feel safe and at home inside my own body only if I could change the world around me. In my days of leading racial reconciliation workshops and facilitating training on racial equity for organizations, my prime objective was to get those around me to act, think, feel, and believe the same way I did. I thought our sameness would be my safety. I thought our agreement would be my resting place. I thought if I could change them, then I'd find peace and satisfaction with being me.

This outward orientation, this fixation on getting others to act, think, feel, and believe differently, had some positive effects. Some people's minds were changed, and some folks' worldviews did expand. What I noticed over time, however, was that the inner conditions of my heart remained largely the same. I still felt overwhelmed and fearful in my body. I still longed for more groundedness and ease in my spirit. I still craved connection, rootedness, and softness, all things that felt unavailable to me as long as I was focused primarily on changing the world. Changing the world out there didn't fix the chaos I felt in my own skin. In response, I turned inward. I started looking at what was in my control and decided to give my best energy there. By turning inward and attending to my own little world, I began experiencing the healing and connection I needed.

Then an unexpected shift occurred. I was a couple years into this inward-focused orientation when I started to experience a sort of disconnect between the good and beautiful life I was creating for myself and the felt, pressing needs of the world around me. In my closest circles, friends were going through faith crises and marriage difficulties. In my local community, nonprofit organizations were in need of volunteers. In the broader cultural and political landscape, countless issues and causes were calling for advocacy and engagement. While I'd constructed my days around a love for slowness, a desire to tend to my body, and contemplative living, all the richness I was personally developing needed an outlet. It needed a place to go, a way to give, an avenue for service. I needed to connect the dots between my own healing and the healing of others.

Around that time, I was invited to facilitate a meeting for a group of leaders convening in Washington, DC. I did all my meeting preparations, boarded a plane to the city, and spent two days with a group of bright and thoughtful people seeking to make the world a better place. To my utter delight and surprise, I loved it. It didn't drain me. I wasn't overwhelmed. I felt focused, clear-eyed, and engaged.

Following the meeting in Washington, DC, I realized that perhaps I'd swung the pendulum too far in the opposite direction from where I'd started. The urgency, anxiety, and fear had become so dreadfully normal that the only solution I could conceive of was to swing as far in the opposite direction as possible, meaning that I'd begun saying no to anything that disturbed my peace or my ability to go slowly. What started as a healthy time of rest, retreat, and recuperation had turned into a self-serving insulation in which I practiced a sort of escape from the world around me. I began to feel restless and disconnected again, but now in a different way. My soul was letting me know it was time to open my heart to the world again.

The Cost of Staying in Crisis Mode

When you're in a cold environment, your fingers and toes get cold first because your body knows, on some level, that in a worst-case scenario, you can live without fingers and toes. But your heart, your lungs, your brain, your inner organs, need more focus, more energy, and more heat, so your body, the brilliant vessel it is, directs more care and support to meet your body's most critical needs. We function in the same way. When resources—time, energy, money, focus, etc.—are scarce, our priorities shift to what needs the most care. When life knocks us down or when traumas from the past begin sounding the alarm for us to attend to them, it makes sense to direct all our mental, physical, and spiritual resources toward the area of our lives that needs the most care and attention.

The tricky part is learning how to come out of crisis mode once the worst of it is over. While staying in crisis mode may seem easier or safer, doing so actually costs us continued growth. It's like remaining in a perpetual winter and never welcoming the newness of spring or the abundance of summer. To remain in the insular state of crisis mode for longer than we need is to build our lives on a foundation of fear. A more beautiful way to live is about welcoming and receiving life as it comes. Life doesn't want us to stay stuck in a fearful, hidden state. Life draws us out into the world and into connection with the aliveness of the world.

How to Open Up Again

Once you've determined it's time to open your heart to the world again, here are three directives to support you in the process:

1. Be honest about your fear.
2. Embrace the risk of living fully.
3. Remember you can always go home.

Be Honest About Your Fear

As is the case with all things, you have to start with reality. If you're afraid to open your heart to the world again, especially after recovering from habits of urgency and anxiety, be honest with yourself about where you are. Your fear is trying to keep you safe, which is a good and necessary protective measure. If you're feeling fearful about opening up your heart to new relationships, opportunities, job offers, or adventures, remind yourself of all the ways you've grown. Let your fear know that you've learned how to embrace slow time when life gets busy. Let your fear know that you've learned how to stop bypassing the needs of your body and how to welcome your body's wisdom to the table. Let your fear know that you've learned how to tend to your inner life so that your mental, emotional, and spiritual health are protected. You have resources now. You have tools in your tool belt that you didn't have before. Remind yourself that it's normal to drop into old habits occasionally but that you now have a pathway back home to yourself and to your values.

You don't have to wait until the fear is gone to step into a new season. Take the fear with you, knowing it's trying to keep you safe. Remind yourself that if you get off course, you have everything you need to return to a more beautiful way.

Embrace the Risk of Living Fully

Opening your heart is always a risk. There are no guarantees. To love, to connect, and to give of yourself to anyone or anything is to put your heart on the line. It involves vulnerability, and it's risky. It's a risk to put yourself out there for professional opportunities with high expectations because there's a chance you could burn out again. There's a risk to communicating your boundaries because people may walk away when you give voice to what you need. It's risky to trust your body again, especially after living through distress or pain. There is always the chance that saying yes to the fullness of your life will lead to falling on your face and having to start over. The beautiful truth is that even if all goes awry, you have the tools and perspective you need to keep learning and growing. Embrace the risk by reminding yourself that the point of healing is to live, not to hide. Embrace the risk by practicing gratitude for all that is going well and right in your world. Embrace the risk by watching the sunrise each morning and letting creation itself remind you that you get to begin again. There is no magic formula for trusting the process that is your ever-unfolding story. You make the decision, again and again, to welcome fresh starts when they come.

Remember You Can Always Go Home

The work it takes to unlearn habits of scatteredness, urgency, and fear and to nurture a lifestyle aimed toward unhurriedness and a receptivity to all that life brings is very similar to paving a path in a forested wilderness. You begin in a wild, disoriented state. You pick up your machete and begin hacking away at the brushes, brambles, and briars in your way. With each step forward, you're creating a path until you reach a clearing. Living a more beautiful way is not just the work of orienting your life; it's also the labor of paving a new path, building your home in the clearing, and creating a place of safety and assurance there.

What's remarkable about wandering in the wilderness and then paving a path to a restful and meaningful place is that now you hold a map. You know the path you carved out by your own hands. You know the rocks you had to move and the briars you had to cut back. You know the fallen tree branches you had to pull out of the way. You know your own history and every ounce of sweat, blood, and tears that got you to a more rooted, sustainable, and beautiful place. You can open your heart to the world now because, no matter what comes, you know the pathway home. It's written in your soul. There may be future wildernesses that will require new tools, new skills, and new maps, but you don't need to worry about getting lost in this specific wilderness again. Remember that you can always go home.

A more beautiful way is sustainable only if you find meaningful ways to give of yourself to the people, places, and causes that need you. As you do so from a place of authenticity and wholeheartedness within yourself, you'll find your energy has a way of regenerating.

I left racial justice education for a time because it was no longer a life-giving expression of my work, but my dedication to the flourishing of African American people and historically marginalized communities has lived on. While I wasn't standing on stages and teaching workshops about racial equity, I had the privilege of participating in a wide array of environmental conservation and economic development efforts supporting rural African American communities. Living a more beautiful way doesn't mean forsaking every part of your former life. It is an invitation to clarify your deeper values so that you can personify them sustainably. The world is in desperate need of people who are rooted enough and resourced enough to participate in the healing of the world without losing connections with their own souls. Your wholeheartedness is integral to lasting justice and transformation in the world around you. May you remain open, engaged, and alive to the good work calling your name.

Nine

LETTING BEAUTY LEAD YOU ON

Many, many years ago, long before dreams of a more beautiful way had materialized in my mind, I found myself walking through a community garden in a refugee resettlement community tended by a group of women from Burundi. The place they were stewarding was nothing short of magical. They'd built their new lives in a country far from their home. They were growing vibrant and nourishing food, and they were sowing richly into a loving and generous web of relationships with their neighbors.

The garden was gorgeous, filled with the bright greens and soft reds of ripening tomatoes as well as the darker greens and deeper reds of bell peppers. The squash and zucchini vines abounded, flowing over the edges of their garden beds. Herbs—basil, oregano, and thyme—were thoughtfully companion-planted throughout. There were also flowers, gorgeous sunflowers and marigolds, bringing the entire space to glorious completion. I was visiting during the best part of summer. It was hot enough for the tomatoes, peppers, okra, and herbs to be in the stage of rapid growth but not so hot as to cause every living thing to wilt under the heavy beating of the late summer sun.

I walked along the mulched pathways and felt my body settle as it hadn't in the longest time. I happened to arrive in this garden in the midst of one of the most challenging seasons of my young adult life. I was a college student, and I was depressed, but I didn't have the language for it at the time. I was overextended but felt as if I couldn't set down any of the responsibilities I was carrying for fear of failure or rejection. I was working incredibly hard and struggling to see the rewards of my labor. I felt isolated and empty on the inside, despite the seeming productivity of my life. Like a tree with shallow roots, I surely would have fallen over with one strong wind.

Seasons of burnout, strain, and disappointment have a way of disconnecting us from our vitality. We wilt from the inside out. "Hope deferred makes the heart sick," says Proverbs 13:12. The burnout and disconnection we feel—the heartsickness that so often gives way to dis-ease in our bodies—signal our need for rejuvenation and care. It is not a failure to need rest, healing, and connection.

When I stepped into the garden that day, my body knew it had entered a place of restoration. My nervous system calmed, and my inner chatter grew quiet. In a way I didn't know I needed, this garden welcomed me home. The mulched pathways, the greenery, the trees. The vegetables, the trellises, the buzzing things. I was at ease in this place. I'd stepped into my forever. It was holy ground. *Salvation.* The beauty of the garden—colorful, awe-inspiring, and pulsing with vibrancy—saved me by giving me a vision worth living toward. This gorgeous, growing green space reminded my soul of what it meant to be alive. When we're on the brink of despondency and despair, nothing hits home quite like nature's unassuming reminders of life itself.

As I walked along the Burundi women's garden path that day, taking in the richness and abundance surrounding me, I noticed a little plaque in one of the garden beds. It said, "Pay attention to what works in the garden, because what works in the garden may one day work in the world." This short turn of phrase echoed in my being. I was captivated by the beauty of the place, and it was as though God spoke directly to my soul, "This garden's goodness is what I want for the entire world."

Compelled by Beauty

Beauty leads us by sparking our hearts and inspiring our minds with possibility. While beauty is equal parts concrete and abstract, touchable and illusive, we all know it when we've seen it.

Jason Baxter, professor of fine arts at Wyoming Catholic College, says this of beauty:

> Being in the presence of . . . beauty doesn't just reverberate with the inner me but also makes me want to pull that best part up and out of me—to strip off all that is superfluous and useless to be the purest, cleanest version of me. By seeing beauty, I want to *be* beauty. When I see beauty, I have this sense that everything can change. I can start over. I can liberate the inner me. . . . I am shocked by beauty, inspired by it, reverberate with it (interiorly), and then [I] resolve to impose more unity on my life (be less disordered) so that I slowly become like what I admire.[1]

Have you ever felt this? Have you perceived something so utterly full of wonder that it evoked a desire in you to become a brighter and more liberated version of who you are? I don't mean the restless perfectionism that drives us to overextend, to pretend, or to perform for love. Nor am I talking about attaining a specific cultural beauty standard or value that holds no real meaning for you. I'm talking about being touched by the spark of divinity in the world and knowing, in your bones, that more life, more joy, and more freedom are possible. It's the inspiration that flows from watching a hummingbird gather nectar. It's the goodness we feel as the ocean tide washes up over our feet. It's the soul-filling delight we know when children roll on the floor in laughter. It's the beauty that leads us on to the most wholehearted and free versions of who we are.

The garden's beauty captivated me that day. Even though it would be years before I began creating a more settled life, I was marked profoundly by the mystically stunning nature of that little patch of cultivated earth. Beauty herself planted a seed in my heart, and while it would take years to grow, it did grow, and I'm living in the abundance of that invitation to pay attention to what works in the garden. Gardens embrace slow time. In fact, slow time is the only time they know. Gardens exist for the nurture of both humans and creatures. Gardens are terrains with boundaries, requiring cultivation and care. Gardens grow and evolve with the seasons. Gardens change as they receive the longings and desires of their caretakers in the form of new plantings and seeds. Gardens welcome times of pruning and of making room for whatever new life is planted therein. A more beautiful way would not exist without the garden as my teacher and my guide.

As you sustain this new way of living for yourself and for the people you're committed to, in what way might beauty be your teacher and your guide? Is there a place you've been that sparked your soul with possibility? Is there an image you've seen that evoked deep desire in you? Perhaps words you've read or sounds you've heard have captivated your senses and reminded your soul of its worth. Wherever you've encountered the beautiful, cherish it. Hold it close to your heart. The world is chaotic, frenzied, rushed, and often full of dread. The truly beautiful can serve as an antidote to the mayhem by compelling you to fix your eyes not on the chaos but on the goodness and inspiration in the created world around you.

How Beauty Helps Us Return

I love beautiful things. Over the years of making a home in rural middle Georgia, I've collected all sorts of tokens and tools whose simple beauty evokes awe and delight in me. There's the beeswax candle set in amber glass whose wooden wick I burn each day as I work. There are the faded, dried hydrangeas resting in a mint green Victorian era vase to the left of my desk. There are my fountain pens and specialty inks positioned so that I can easily see and enjoy all their colors at all times. There are the art prints of designers and illustrators whose work inspires me asymmetrically hung across my office walls. I have made it a point to surround myself with items I find beautiful because their concrete expressions of coherence and design bring peace and comfort to my soul.

The beauty of the natural world has a similar effect on our souls in that it can serve as a tangible expression of order and intention, which can help bring focus and direction to our inner lives. On tough days when the news is heavy and hope is hard to come by, I look out my window and see the eastern red cedar standing tall and firm, with branches expanding, bearing juniper berries in season and providing shelter for the birds. I see the tree's magnificence, and I'm struck by how steady and assured it is. It's as though the tree itself reminds my inner world that living beings were created to stand confidently, to be firmly rooted in who they are, to bear good fruit, and to provide care for one another. All throughout the natural world are reminders of what it is to lead a grounded, present life. Our job, when we find ourselves pulled off the path by the difficulties and distractions life brings, is to let the beautiful serve as a gentle nudge to return to the more beautiful way we've been living.

When life feels overwhelming and when I'm struck with fear of what the future may bring, the delightful tools and tokens in my home and in the natural world help me return to a rooted, connected, and soul-filling way of being in the world. They are concrete, helping me get out of my head and into my body's felt experience. They are well-designed, bringing emotional peace and intellectual clarity to my often-cluttered mind. They are colorful, validating the rich diversity and complexity of the human experience. And as for the created world, it is always changing, teaching me that variation and adaptation are part and parcel of the process of being alive.

What do you find beautiful? It can be an item or collection of items; it can be artwork or music. It can be a grandly constructed building or an astonishing landscape. Name what you find beautiful so that you have a guiding inspiration to help you find your way back to the path when life obscures the way. If you aren't sure what qualifies as beautiful for you, feel free to borrow my conditions. I know the beautiful to be:

- Concrete, meaning it is tangible. I can touch it or feel it or smell it. I can be immersed in an experience of it with all my senses, which helps me be embodied.
- Designed, meaning it is crafted with intention. It has a purpose and an order, which is tremendously comforting.
- Colorful, meaning it captures a wide array of the light spectrum, sparking my own creativity and desire for variety.
- Adaptive, meaning it evolves, bends, contracts, and expands with the progression of time.

Take a few moments now to consider what you find beautiful. Once you have a response or a few, write them down on a piece of paper or in a journal. Consider how you might integrate more of that beauty into your daily life. Is there a token you can place in a prominent spot in your home? Is there an image you can set as the background of your phone? What you find beautiful will serve as a beacon when the path before you grows dim and you need to find your way back to living a more beautiful way.

I stood at the top of the trail and peered down the long, muddy slope toward a waterfall in the distance. I could hear the water rushing over the edge of a cliff and crashing into the pool below. It roared, majestic and overflowing. Even from a distance, I knew it was a sight worth seeing up close.

The trail, however, was intimidating. It seemed to be a direct drop-off, vertically descending into unknown territory. There was no built infrastructure—no rails, no stairs, no sturdy planks to guide you down into the gorge. There were only ropes. Lots of ropes with knots for holding were tied to the strongest trees and anchor points every ten feet or so all the way down the side of the mountain. I was starting to think that getting down to the falls was impossible when I caught a glimpse of four gray-haired women, slowly and in support of one another, clinging to the ropes as they hiked back up the mountain's side to the top of the trail where I was standing. *If they can do it, then surely I have no excuse*, I thought to myself.

Alex and I exchanged curious glances and excited chatter as we debated whether the hike was worth it. He was eager and kept saying, "Let's just try it." I was nervous and kept saying, "I didn't sign up for this today." But the truth is I'd follow him anywhere, and I really did want to see the majesty of the falls below. He began making his way down the mountain; I rolled up my jeans, took a deep breath, grabbed the first rope, and began the descent.

I took my time. The path was boggy and slippery in more than one place. There were multiple points where I just had to stand still and think about how I wanted to move forward. *Should I place my foot here or there? Should I get lower to the ground? Maybe I need Alex's hand to steady me on this next part . . .* but I kept going. It was as though the laurel bushes growing along the sides of the mountain cheered me on as I persisted on this new adventure.

As I continued my descent into the gorge, the roar of the falls grew louder and louder. Before I knew it, we were there, standing on the edge of a deep blue-green pool of ice-cold water, churning under the force of a fifty-foot waterfall. We were in a sort of paradise. It was magical. I settled down on a large rock directly across from the falls and took it all in. Spring was just beginning, meaning the trees around us were mostly bare but had begun setting their buds to bloom in a few weeks' time. The bareness of the trees made it easy for sunlight to break through. The sun's rays kissed the waterfall, the mountain wall, and my cheeks as I bathed in the vibrancy of the moment. I sat there in stillness and quiet, feeling alive and proud and deeply satisfied to have taken this unexpected trek into the heart of this mountainside. I knew the day's adventure would mark me for many years to come.

A more beautiful way to live is a trek into the heart of your life. Much of the journey is boggy and messy. Making the descent into this place within requires inspiration and guidance. It takes courage to face limiting beliefs, to ask for help, and to tend to your pain. It takes self-awareness and a strong knowledge of your body to move at a pace that keeps you advancing even when the trail becomes slippery or feels insecure. And perhaps more than anything, you must be able to hear your soul's longing, like the waterfall's roar, drawing you further down and deeper in, all in hopes of reaching that magical, sun-kissed place of sustenance and true rest. After you reach this place, the invitation is to now live from this place. Live each and every day, as you are able, with an eye toward being firmly rooted, fully in the present moment, and strengthened in your ability to receive and accept life as it comes your way. Slowing down will help you on this path. Learning from nature and living with the seasons will anchor you as you mark time in new ways. Rhythms of ritual will help you find your way back to the pathway when you get lost.

Living a more beautiful way may seem intimidating, if not impossible, while standing at the top of the trail, peering over the edge toward the way you're longing for most. But know that the practices explored here, like the ropes and their knots, will hold you up as you descend. Know that others have taken this path before, have survived it, and are joyfully telling the tale. And know that while your body may grow tired and your spirit may grow faint, if you keep going, there is a sacred wellspring of connection, wholeheartedness, and resilience waiting for you.

PAUSE & REFLECT

You made it! Welcome to the next phase of living a more beautiful way. While my guidance in this book has come to an end, your work continues. My hope for you in the coming days, months, and years is that the exercises and reflections found here deepen in their effectiveness as you practice them. Creating rituals will help you sustainably integrate slowness, connection to your body, and awareness of your inner terrain into your lived experience. Learning how to remain openhearted to the world, though challenging, will steadily invite you to give your time, energy, and skill to the people you're called to serve. Letting beauty guide you will remind your soul of its worth on the days when leading a life of groundedness and intention feels just out of reach. Here are a few final reflection questions to support you in sustaining a more beautiful way of life for the long haul.

On Nourishing Your Life Through Rituals

1. Review the collection of daily, weekly, monthly, and annual rituals proposed in this chapter. Which rituals, if any, would you like to incorporate into your life? What will it take to ensure these rituals are prioritized?
2. How would you describe your relationship with *play*? What, if anything, surprises you about your response?

3. When was the last time you stepped outside of the normal rhythm of your life and dreamed about your future? What was the experience like? How did it impact you?

On Opening Your Heart to the World

1. How do you know when you're living in crisis mode? What are the signs? What helps you transition out of crisis mode?
2. What does *living fully* mean to you?
3. What community needs or social causes are most important to you? What might it look like for you to lend your time, energy, and skill to meet those needs or address those causes?

On Letting Beauty Lead You On

1. When was the last time you encountered something truly beautiful? How would you describe it? What impact did it have on you?
2. What inspires you? What gives you hope?
3. What does "a more beautiful way" mean to you?

ACKNOWLEDGMENTS

My gratitude abounds for the place that held me as I wrote this book. We call it Cedar Wilde, the one-acre parcel of land nestled between cattle fields and carved out of the forest. I know it may be strange to thank a place for helping me tell this story, but Cedar Wilde has been with me each step of the way. For this place, I am grateful.

Thank you to my editor, Grace P. Cho, for believing in me and for drawing me deeper into my own story, even when I was grief-filled and afraid.

Thank you to my agent, Chris Ferebee, for saying yes to journeying with me through another book adventure.

Thank you to my many, many teachers from the past few years whose wisdom and practice have anchored my life—namely, Danielle Lyles Barton, Hailey Mitsui, Jazzy Johnson, Erna Kim Hackett, Courtnee Wilson, Jessica Hogan, Margaret Reynolds, Siedeh Foxie, Mary Claire Coleman, Laura Green, Lindsay Mack, Erin Rose Belair, Laura Stemmer, Jade Moyano, and my entire spiritual direction cohort from the Parish Resource Center.

Thank you to my family and ancestors for teaching me to love the land.

And thank you to my love, Alex Wilkinson, for walking with me through every season life has brought our way.

I would also like to thank the readers who follow and support my work on Instagram and Substack. Your receptivity and responsiveness as I've shared vulnerably throughout my journey have given me courage and confidence to keep writing and to keep sharing the lessons I'm learning. Thank you for reading and for doing your part to cultivate beauty in our world.

NOTES

Foreword

1. Clarissa Pinkola Estés, "Do Not Lose Heart, We Were Made for These Times," DailyGood, March 13, 2020, https://www.dailygood.org/story/1538/do-not-lose-heart-we-were-made-for-these-times-clarissa-pinkola-estes/.

Introducing a More Beautiful Way to Live

1. *Merriam-Webster Dictionary*, "time," accessed February 1, 2025, https://www.merriam-webster.com/dictionary/time.

Chapter 1 Embracing Slow Time

1. Brené Brown, *The Gifts of Imperfection: Let Go of Who You Think You're Supposed to Be and Embrace Who You Are* (Hazelden, 2022), 94.
2. Richard Rohr, *Everything Belongs: The Gift of Contemplative Prayer* (Crossroad, 2003), 75.

Chapter 2 Connecting with Your Body

1. Hillary McBride, *The Wisdom of Your Body: Finding Healing, Wholeness, and Connection Through Embodied Living* (Brazos, 2021), 16.
2. Sebastian Conrad, "Enlightenment in Global History: A Historiographical Critique," *American Historical Review* (October 1, 2012): 117.
3. Niva Piran, *Journeys of Embodiment at the Intersection of Body and Culture: The Developmental Theory of Embodiment* (Elsevier, 2017), 6.
4. McBride, *Wisdom of Your Body*, 15.

Chapter 3 Awakening to Your Inner Terrain

1. Parker J. Palmer, *A Hidden Wholeness: The Journey Toward an Undivided Life: Welcoming the Soul and Weaving Community in a Wounded World* (Jossey-Bass, 2009), 58.

2. David G. Benner, *The Gift of Being Yourself: The Sacred Call to Self-Discovery* (InterVarsity, 2015), 24.

3. *Online Etymological Dictionary*, "fractal," accessed June 10, 2025, https://www.etymonline.com/word/fractal.

4. Dexter Johnson, "Mimicking the Veins in a Leaf, Scientists Hope to Make Super-Efficient Displays and Solar Cells," September 30, 2016, https://spectrum.ieee.org/mimicking-the-veins-in-a-leaf-researchers-make-super-efficient-displays-and-solar-cells.

5. Stephen Covey, *The Seven Habits of Highly Effective People: Powerful Lessons in Personal Change* (Simon & Schuster, 2020), 88.

Chapter 4 Living with the Seasons

1. Katherine May, *Wintering: The Power of Rest and Retreat in Difficult Times* (Riverhead Books, 2020), 14.

2. Colin Murray Parkes, *Bereavement: Studies of Grief in Adult Life* (Routledge, 1972), chap. 1, Kindle.

3. *Merriam-Webster Dictionary*, "taproot," accessed July 29, 2025, https://www.merriam-webster.com/dictionary/taproot.

4. Jean Lengacher, "Contemplative Prayer Guide," email to Kairos Spiritual Direction Cohort, November 2023.

Chapter 5 Listening for Your Longings

1. Bethaney Wilkinson, host, *A More Beautiful Way* podcast, season 1, episode 3, "Art Is Medicine and Sending Flowers to Greenwood," with Leah Palmer, August 24, 2023, https://www.amorebeautifulway.co/p/03-art-is-medicine-and-sending-flowers-6d8.

2. *Online Etymology Dictionary*, "discern," accessed July 29, 2025, https://www.etymonline.com/word/discern.

3. Elizabeth Liebert, *The Way of Discernment: Spiritual Practices for Decision Making* (Westminster John Knox, 2008), 8.

Chapter 7 Nourishing Your Life Through Rituals

1. *Merriam-Webster Dictionary*, "ritual," accessed February 27, 2025, https://www.merriam-webster.com/dictionary/ritual.

2. Julia Cameron, *The Artist's Way* (TarcherPerigee, 2016), 10.

3. This information can be accessed at https://www.sdicompanions.org.

4. Kendra Cherry, "Negativity Bias: Why We're Hardwired for Negativity," Verywell Mind, November 13, 2023, https://www.verywellmind.com/negative-bias-4589618.

Chapter 9 Letting Beauty Lead You On

1. Jason Baxter, *An Introduction to Christian Mysticism: Recovering the Wildness of Spiritual Life* (Baker Academic, 2021), 57.

BETHANEY WILKINSON is a writer, facilitator, and spiritual director rooted in rural middle Georgia, where she lives with her husband Alex and their two dogs, Isla and Bear. She has an MA in theology from Fuller Theological Seminary and a BA in educational studies from Emory University. She is also the author of *The Diversity Gap: Where Good Intentions Meet True Cultural Change*.

Connect with Bethaney:

www.bethaneywilkinson.com

INSTAGRAM @bethaney.bree

THREADS @bethaney.bree

SUBSTACK www.amorebeautifulway.co